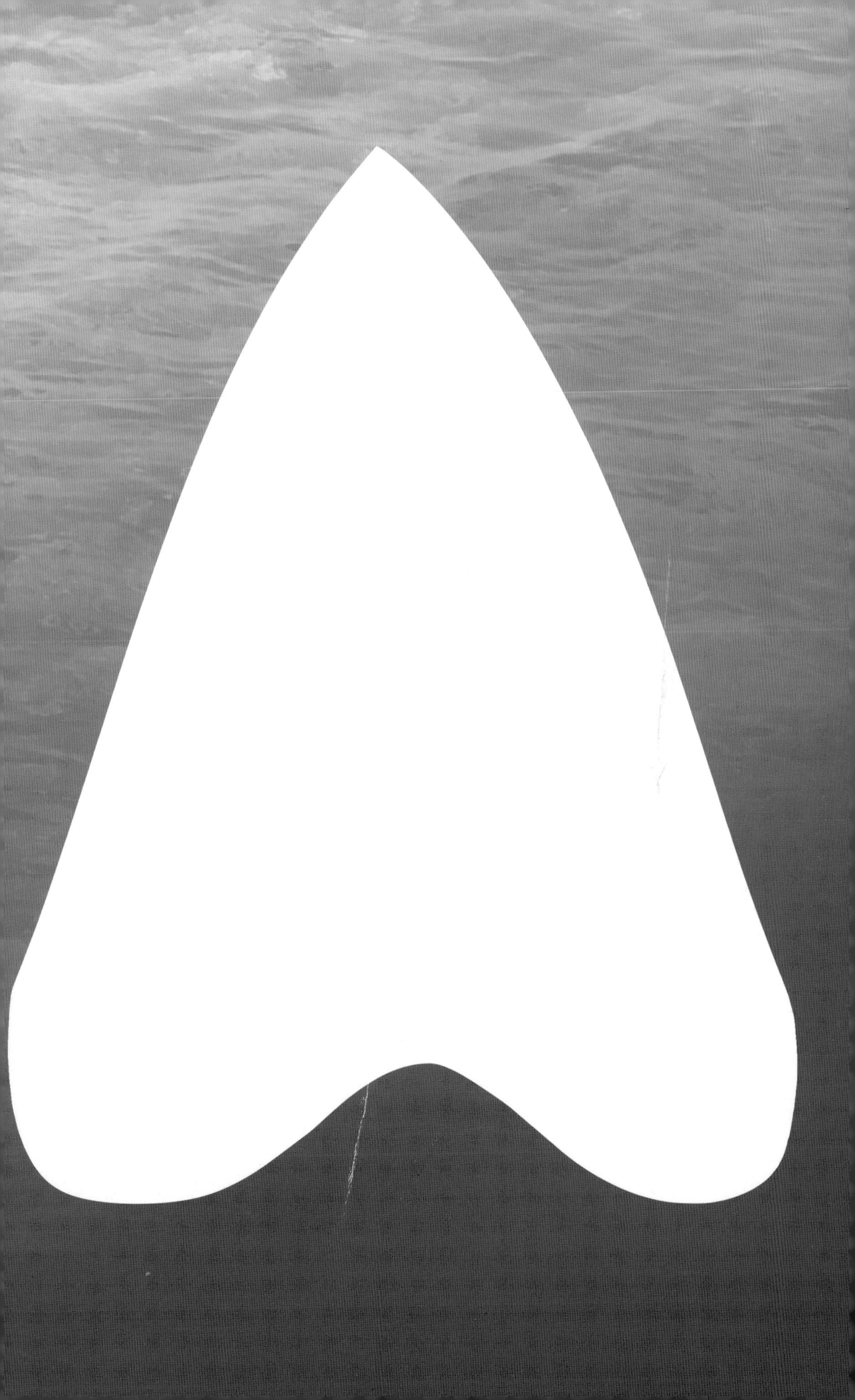

REXTOOTH
STUDIOS

SHARKS

WRITTEN & ILLUSTRATED BY **TED RECHLIN**

EDITOR **ANNE RECHLIN**

PUBLISHED BY REXTOOTH STUDIOS, BOZEMAN, MONTANA

PRODUCED BY SWEETGRASS BOOKS, HELENA, MONTANA

ISBN: 978-1-59152-213-3

COVER DESIGN BY TED RECHLIN

PRODUCED IN THE UNITED STATES OF AMERICA

PRINTED IN CHINA

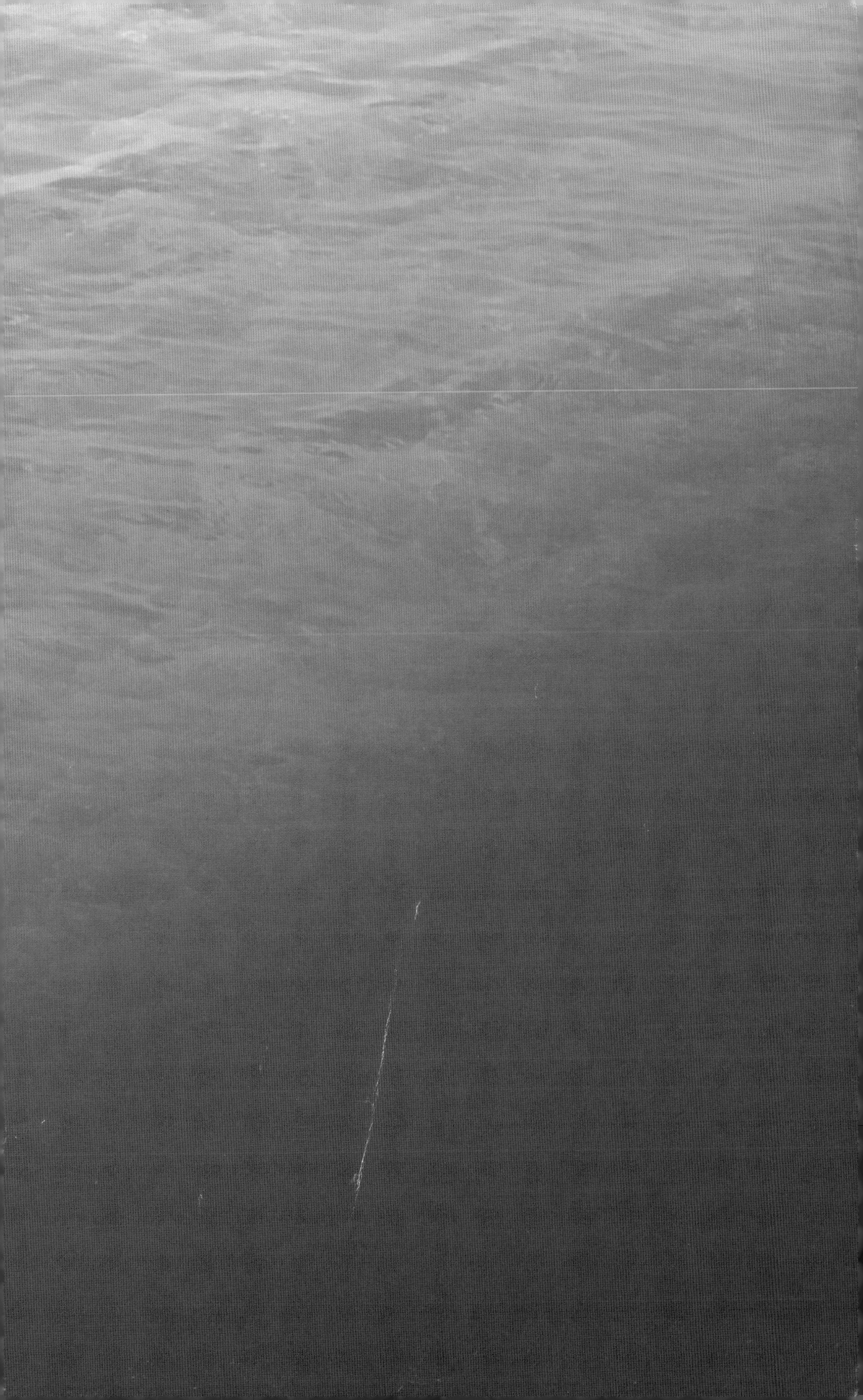

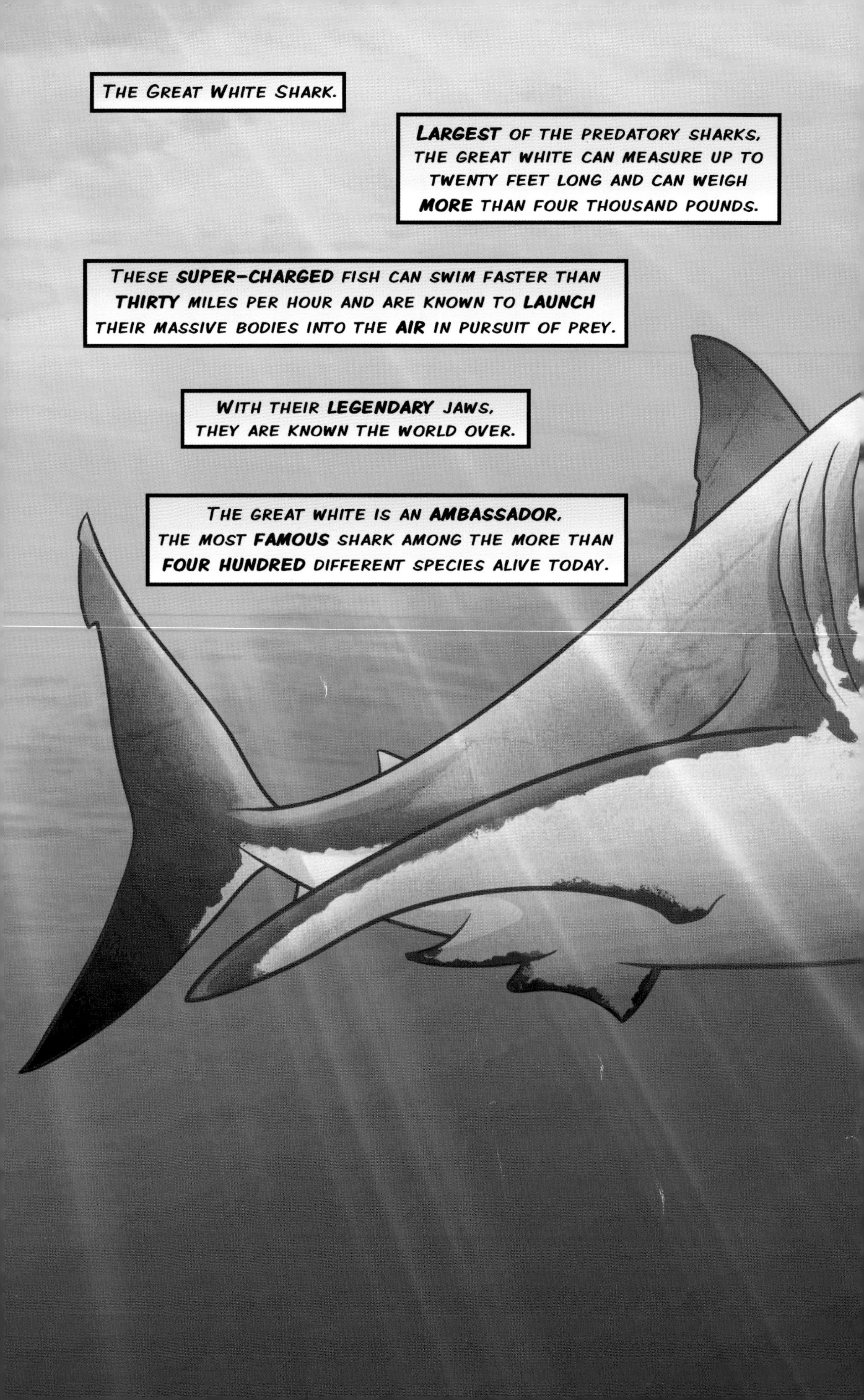

THE GREAT WHITE SHARK.
LARGEST OF THE PREDATORY SHARKS, THE GREAT WHITE CAN MEASURE UP TO TWENTY FEET LONG AND CAN WEIGH MORE THAN FOUR THOUSAND POUNDS.
THESE SUPER-CHARGED FISH CAN SWIM FASTER THAN THIRTY MILES PER HOUR AND ARE KNOWN TO LAUNCH THEIR MASSIVE BODIES INTO THE AIR IN PURSUIT OF PREY.
WITH THEIR LEGENDARY JAWS, THEY ARE KNOWN THE WORLD OVER.
THE GREAT WHITE IS AN AMBASSADOR, THE MOST FAMOUS SHARK AMONG THE MORE THAN FOUR HUNDRED DIFFERENT SPECIES ALIVE TODAY.

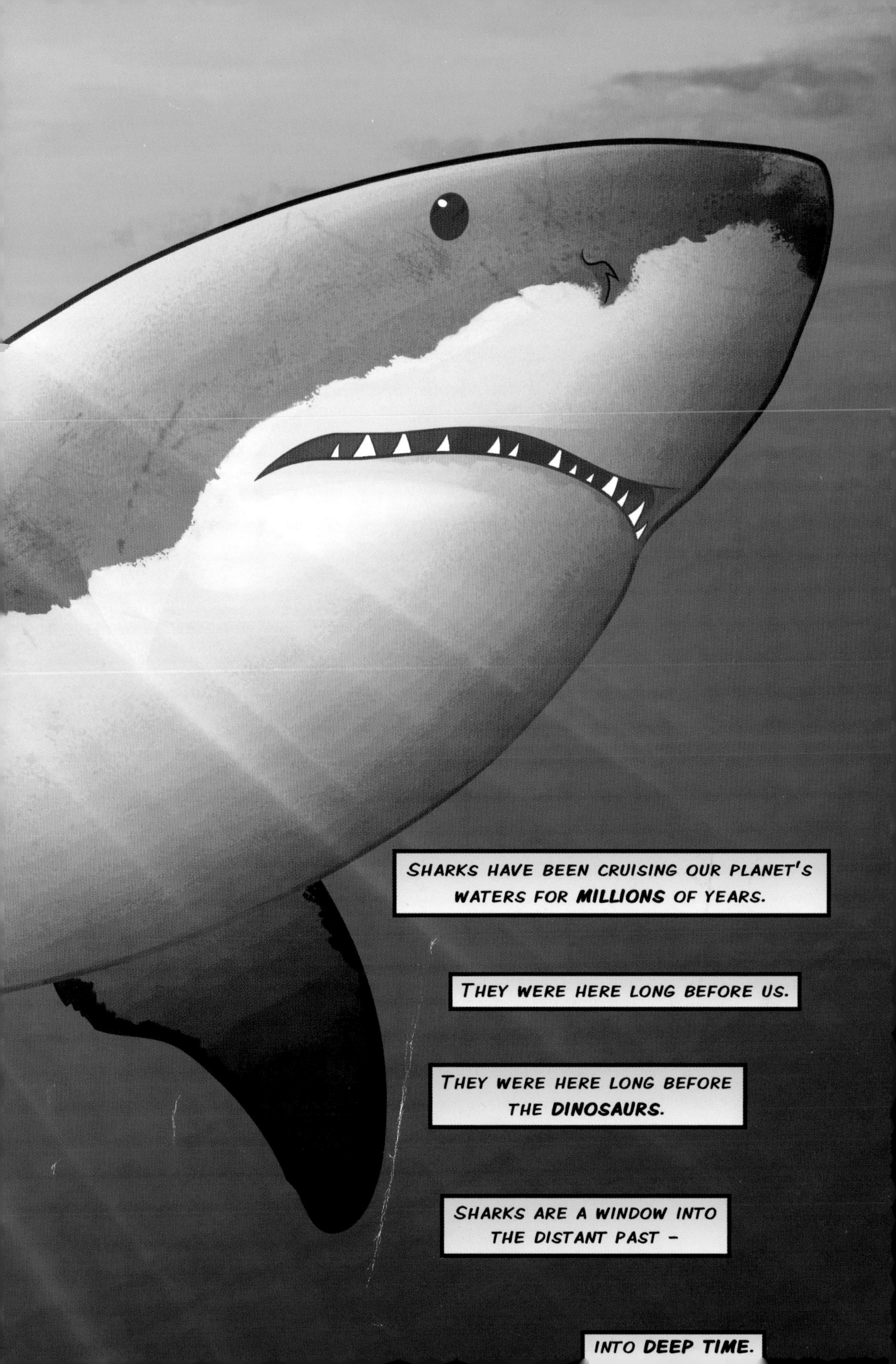
SHARKS HAVE BEEN CRUISING OUR PLANET'S WATERS FOR MILLIONS OF YEARS.
THEY WERE HERE LONG BEFORE US.
THEY WERE HERE LONG BEFORE THE DINOSAURS.
SHARKS ARE A WINDOW INTO THE DISTANT PAST -
INTO DEEP TIME.

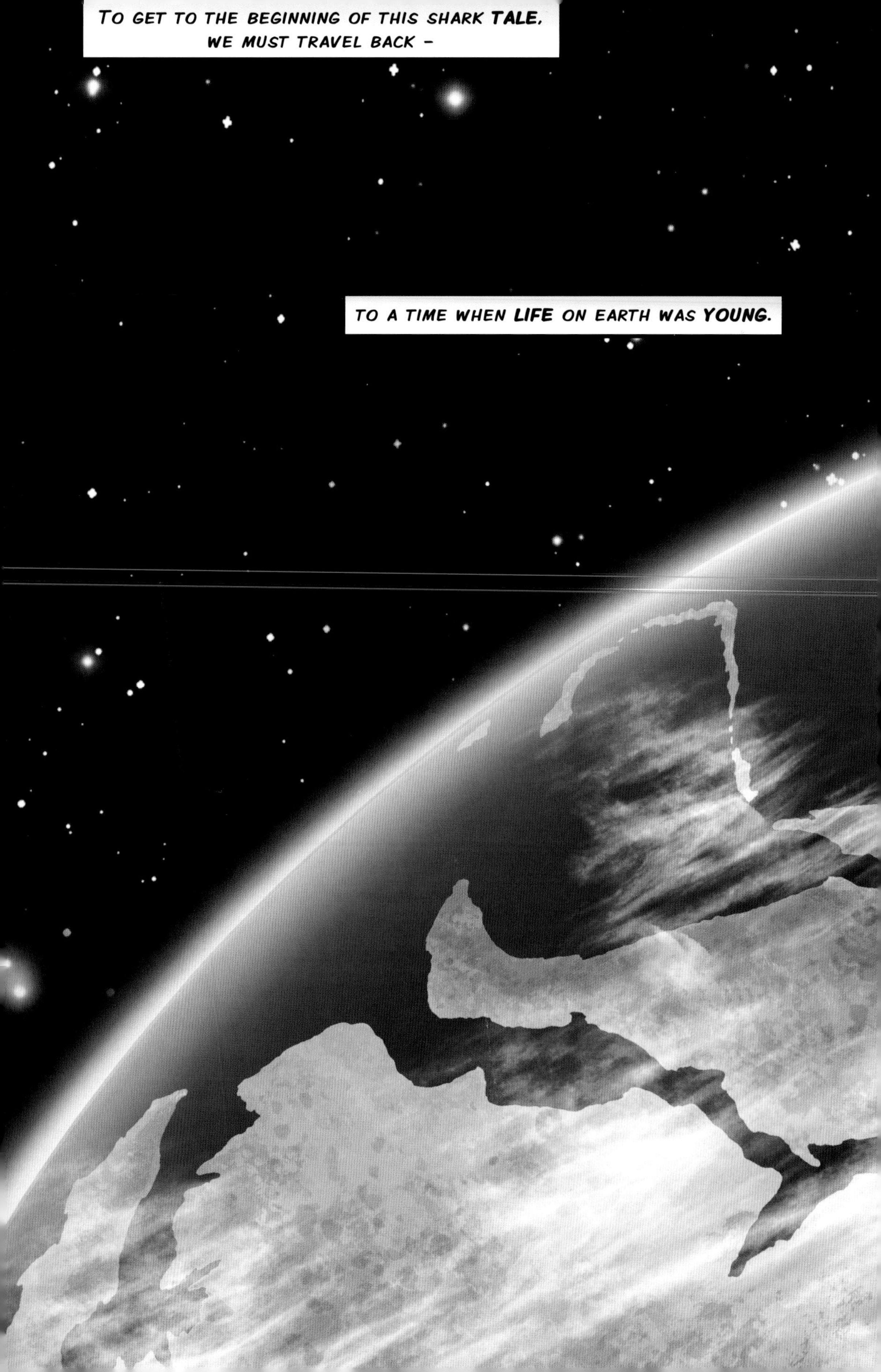
TO GET TO THE BEGINNING OF THIS SHARK TALE, WE MUST TRAVEL BACK -
TO A TIME WHEN LIFE ON EARTH WAS YOUNG.

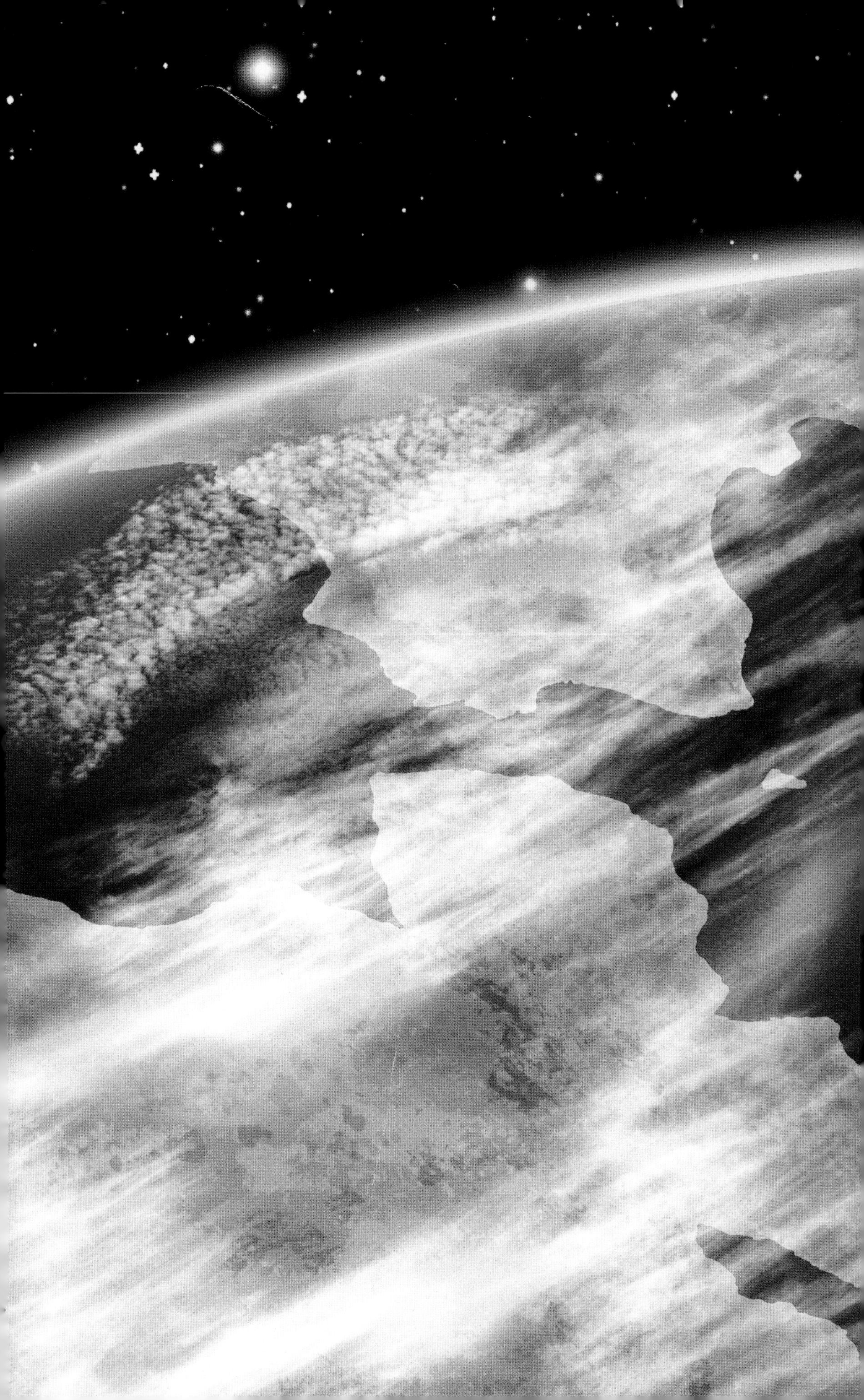

PART ONE
PALEOZOIC

541 - 252
MILLION YEARS AGO

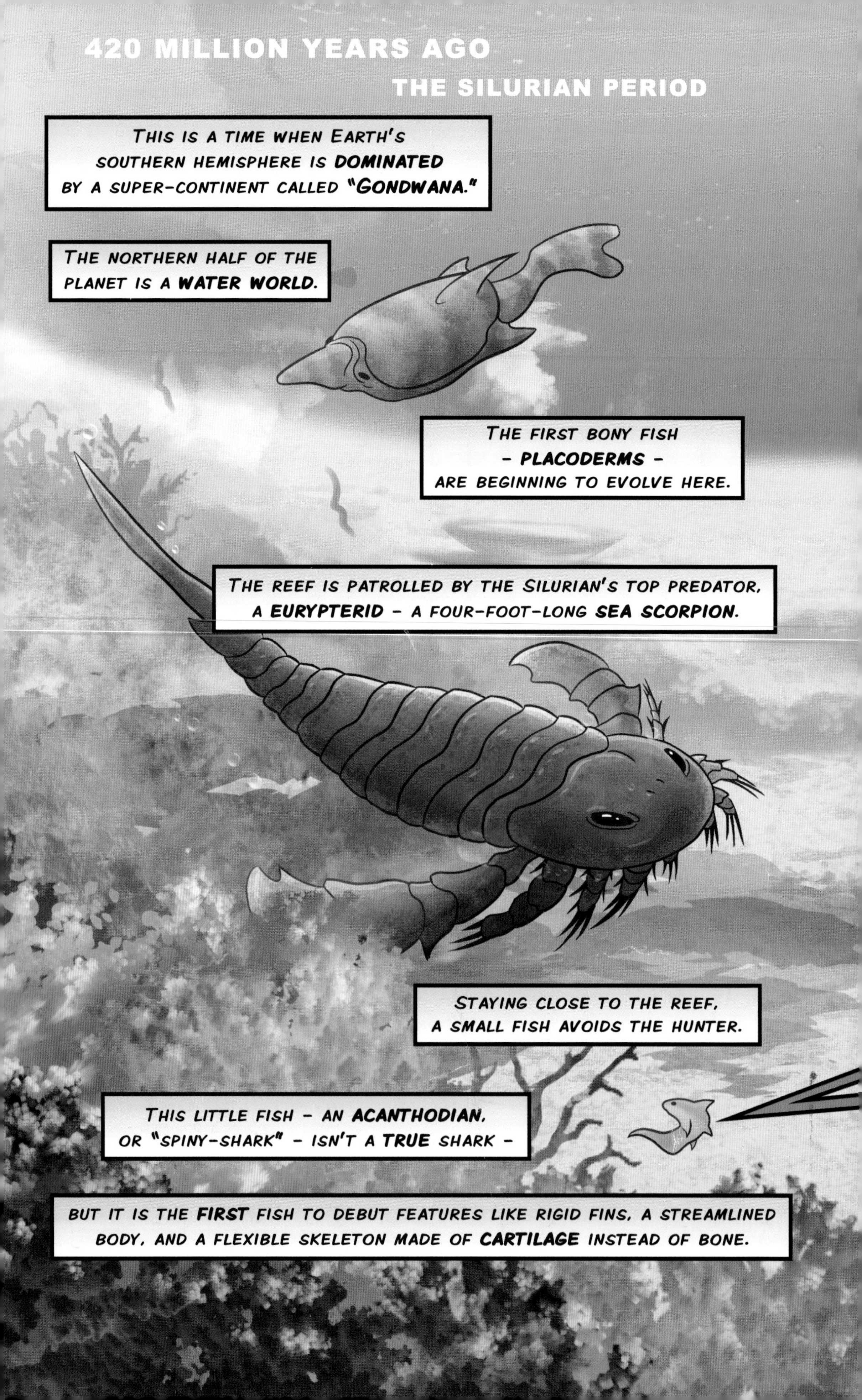
420 MILLION YEARS AGO
THE SILURIAN PERIOD
THIS IS A TIME WHEN EARTH'S SOUTHERN HEMISPHERE IS DOMINATED BY A SUPER-CONTINENT CALLED "GONDWANA."
THE NORTHERN HALF OF THE PLANET IS A WATER WORLD.
THE FIRST BONY FISH - PLACODERMS - ARE BEGINNING TO EVOLVE HERE.
THE REEF IS PATROLLED BY THE SILURIAN'S TOP PREDATOR, A EURYPTERID - A FOUR-FOOT-LONG SEA SCORPION.
STAYING CLOSE TO THE REEF, A SMALL FISH AVOIDS THE HUNTER.
THIS LITTLE FISH - AN ACANTHODIAN, OR "SPINY-SHARK" - ISN'T A TRUE SHARK -
BUT IT IS THE FIRST FISH TO DEBUT FEATURES LIKE RIGID FINS, A STREAMLINED BODY, AND A FLEXIBLE SKELETON MADE OF CARTILAGE INSTEAD OF BONE.

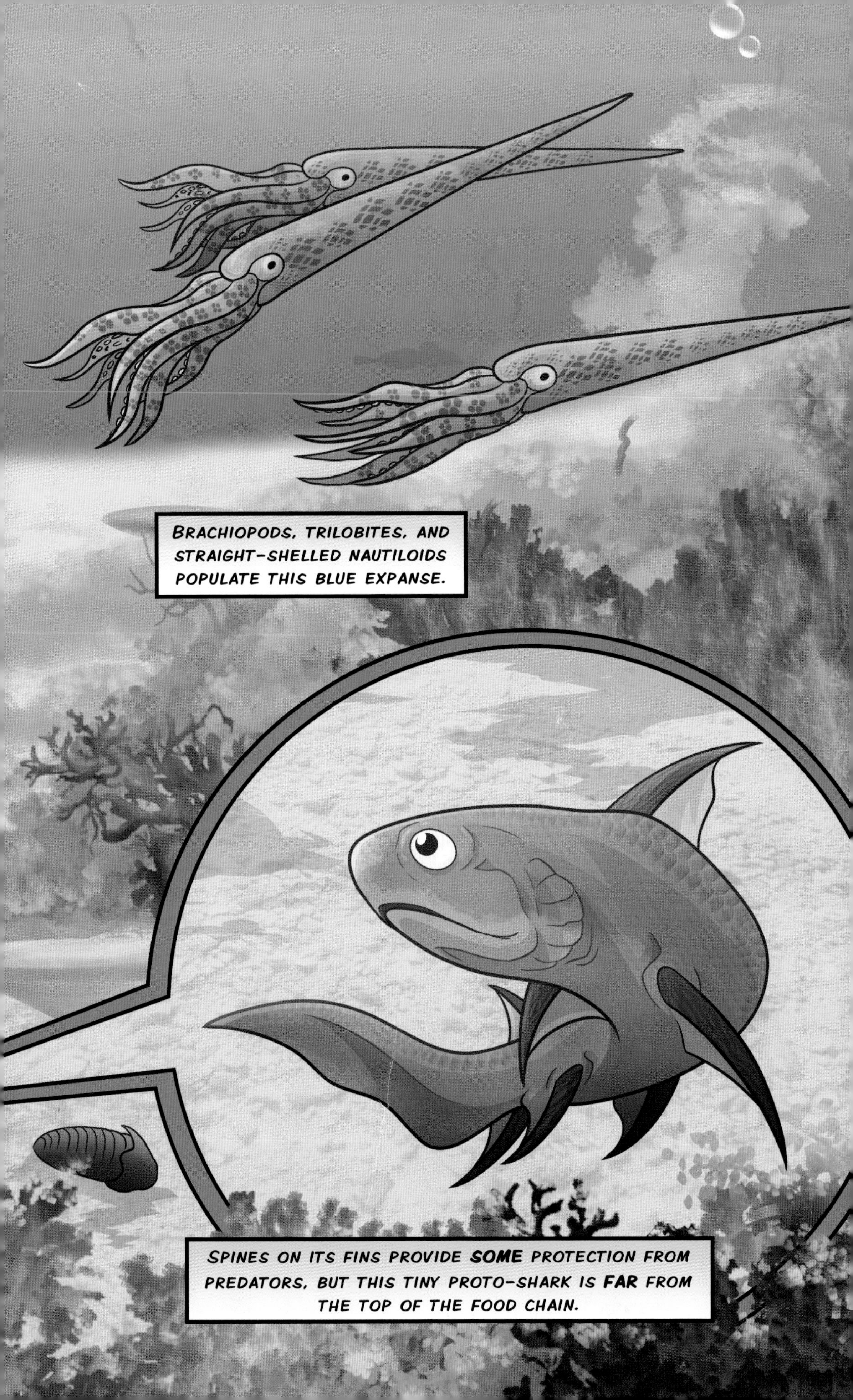
BRACHIOPODS, TRILOBITES, AND STRAIGHT-SHELLED NAUTILOIDS POPULATE THIS BLUE EXPANSE.
SPINES ON ITS FINS PROVIDE **SOME** PROTECTION FROM PREDATORS, BUT THIS TINY PROTO-SHARK IS **FAR** FROM THE TOP OF THE FOOD CHAIN.

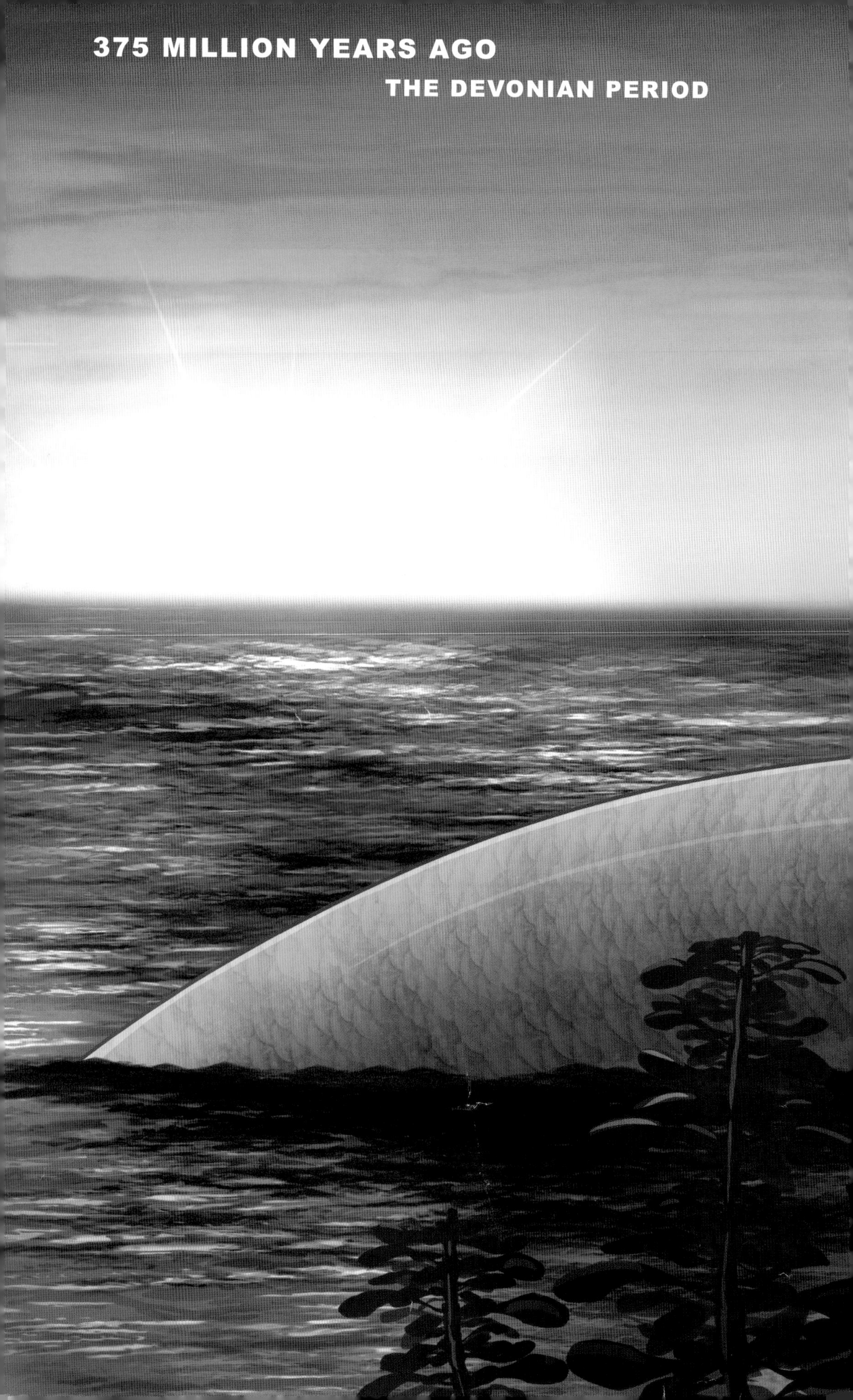
375 MILLION YEARS AGO
THE DEVONIAN PERIOD

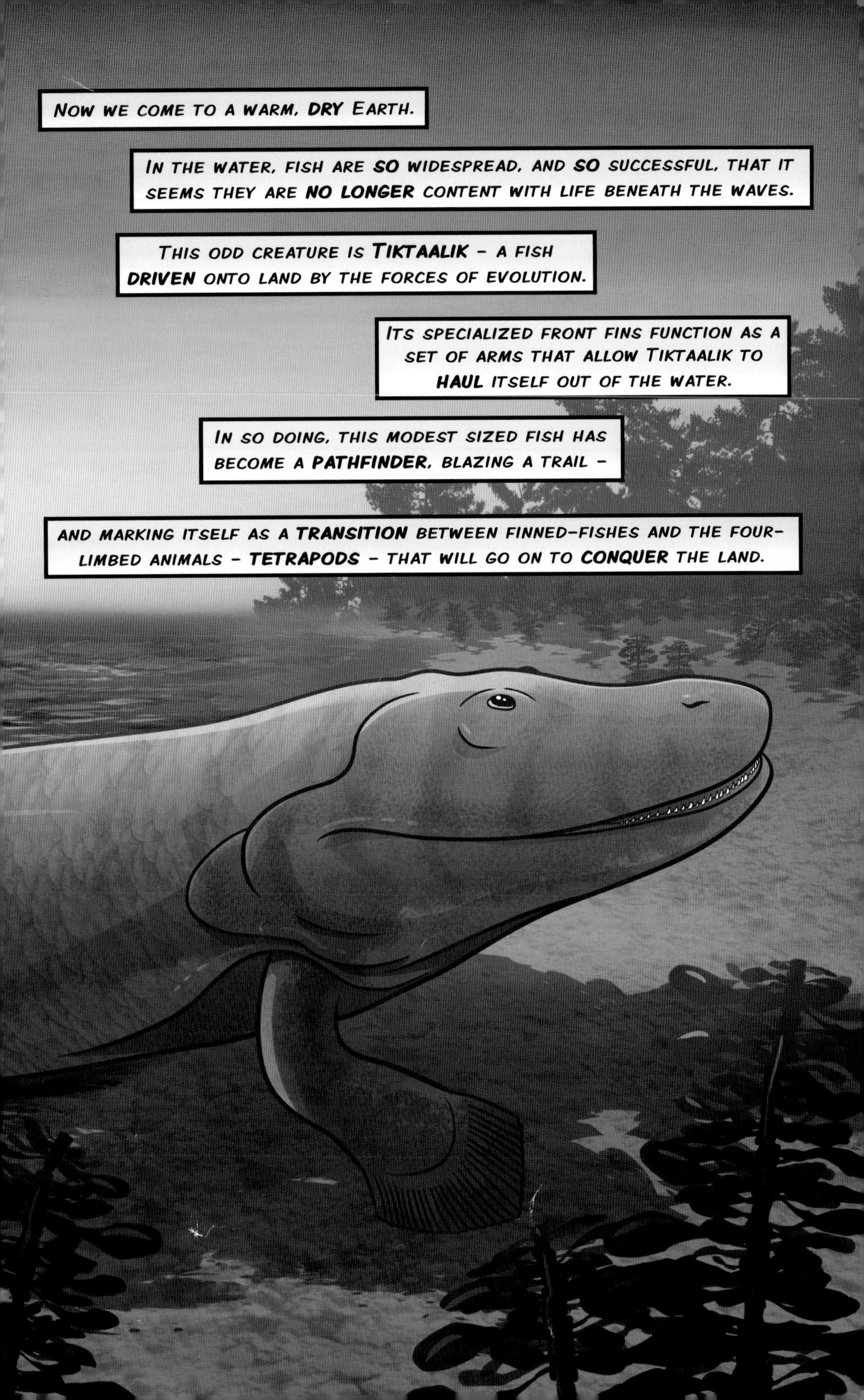
NOW WE COME TO A WARM, DRY EARTH.
IN THE WATER, FISH ARE SO WIDESPREAD, AND SO SUCCESSFUL, THAT IT SEEMS THEY ARE NO LONGER CONTENT WITH LIFE BENEATH THE WAVES.
THIS ODD CREATURE IS TIKTAALIK - A FISH DRIVEN ONTO LAND BY THE FORCES OF EVOLUTION.
ITS SPECIALIZED FRONT FINS FUNCTION AS A SET OF ARMS THAT ALLOW TIKTAALIK TO HAUL ITSELF OUT OF THE WATER.
IN SO DOING, THIS MODEST SIZED FISH HAS BECOME A PATHFINDER, BLAZING A TRAIL -
AND MARKING ITSELF AS A TRANSITION BETWEEN FINNED-FISHES AND THE FOUR-LIMBED ANIMALS - TETRAPODS - THAT WILL GO ON TO CONQUER THE LAND.

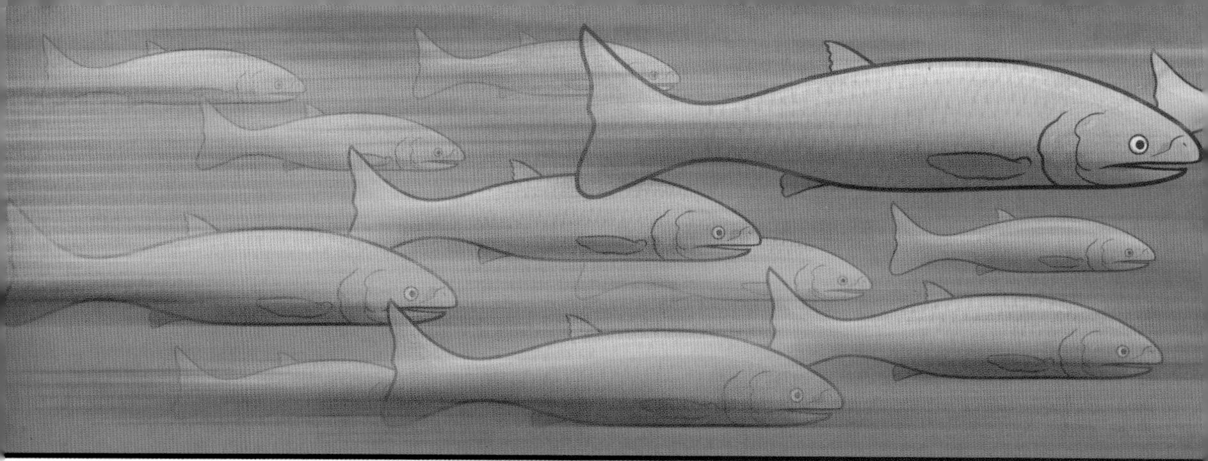

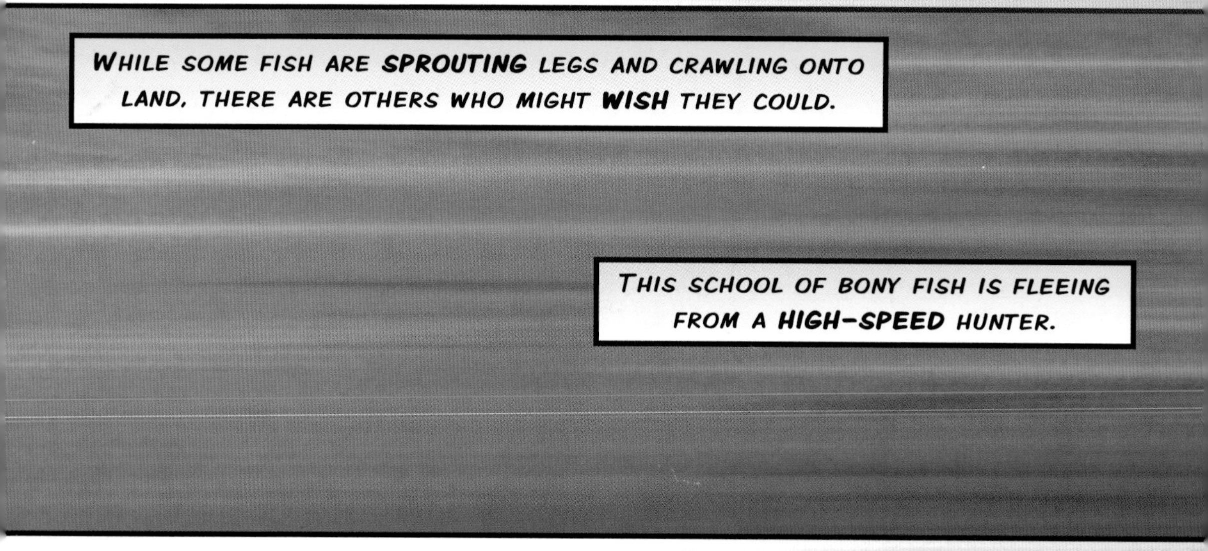
WHILE SOME FISH ARE SPROUTING LEGS AND CRAWLING ONTO LAND, THERE ARE OTHERS WHO MIGHT WISH THEY COULD.
THIS SCHOOL OF BONY FISH IS FLEEING FROM A HIGH-SPEED HUNTER.

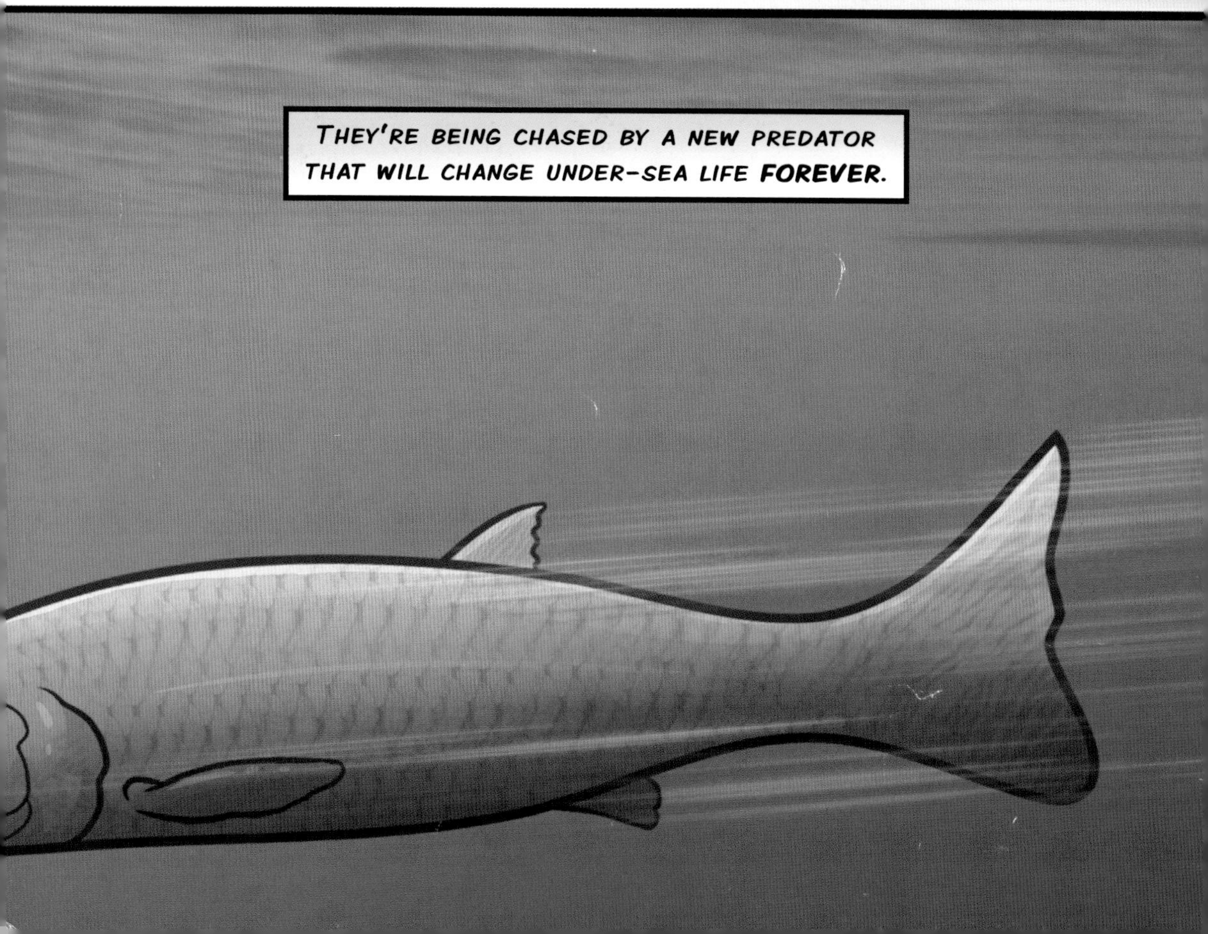
THEY'RE BEING CHASED BY A NEW PREDATOR THAT WILL CHANGE UNDER-SEA LIFE FOREVER.

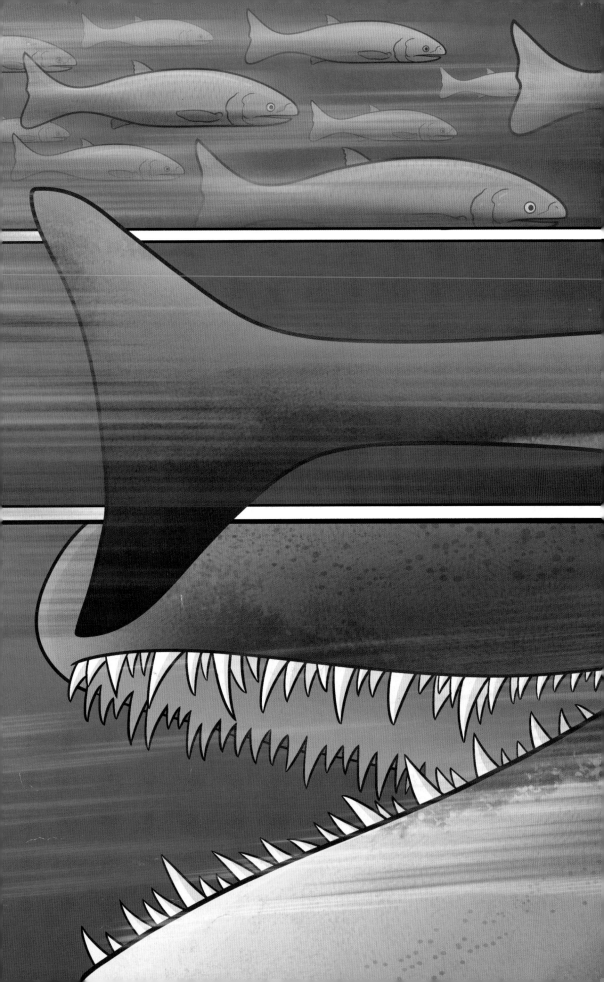

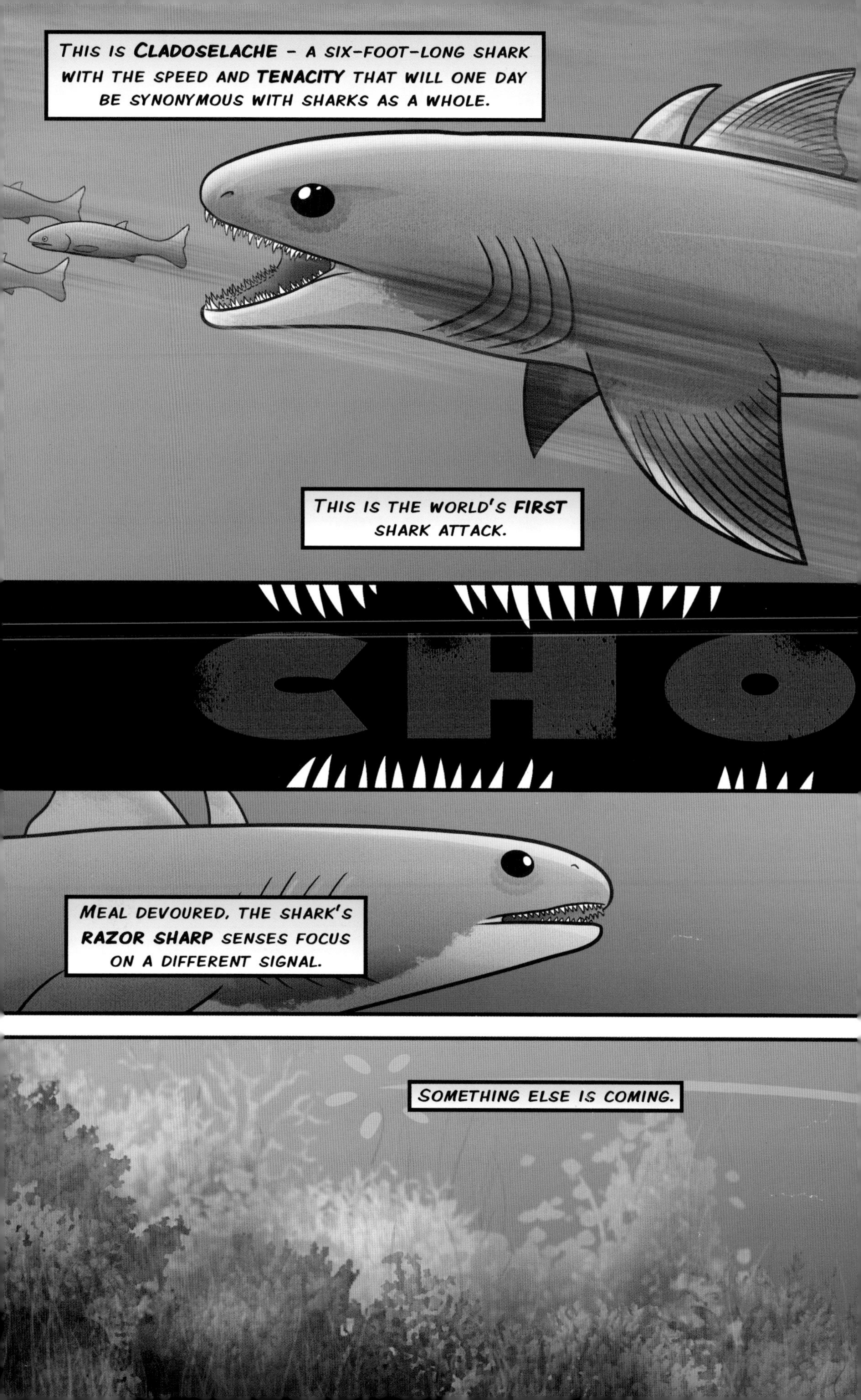
THIS IS CLADOSELACHE - A SIX-FOOT-LONG SHARK WITH THE SPEED AND TENACITY THAT WILL ONE DAY BE SYNONYMOUS WITH SHARKS AS A WHOLE.
THIS IS THE WORLD'S FIRST SHARK ATTACK.
CHO
MEAL DEVOURED, THE SHARK'S RAZOR SHARP SENSES FOCUS ON A DIFFERENT SIGNAL.
SOMETHING ELSE IS COMING.

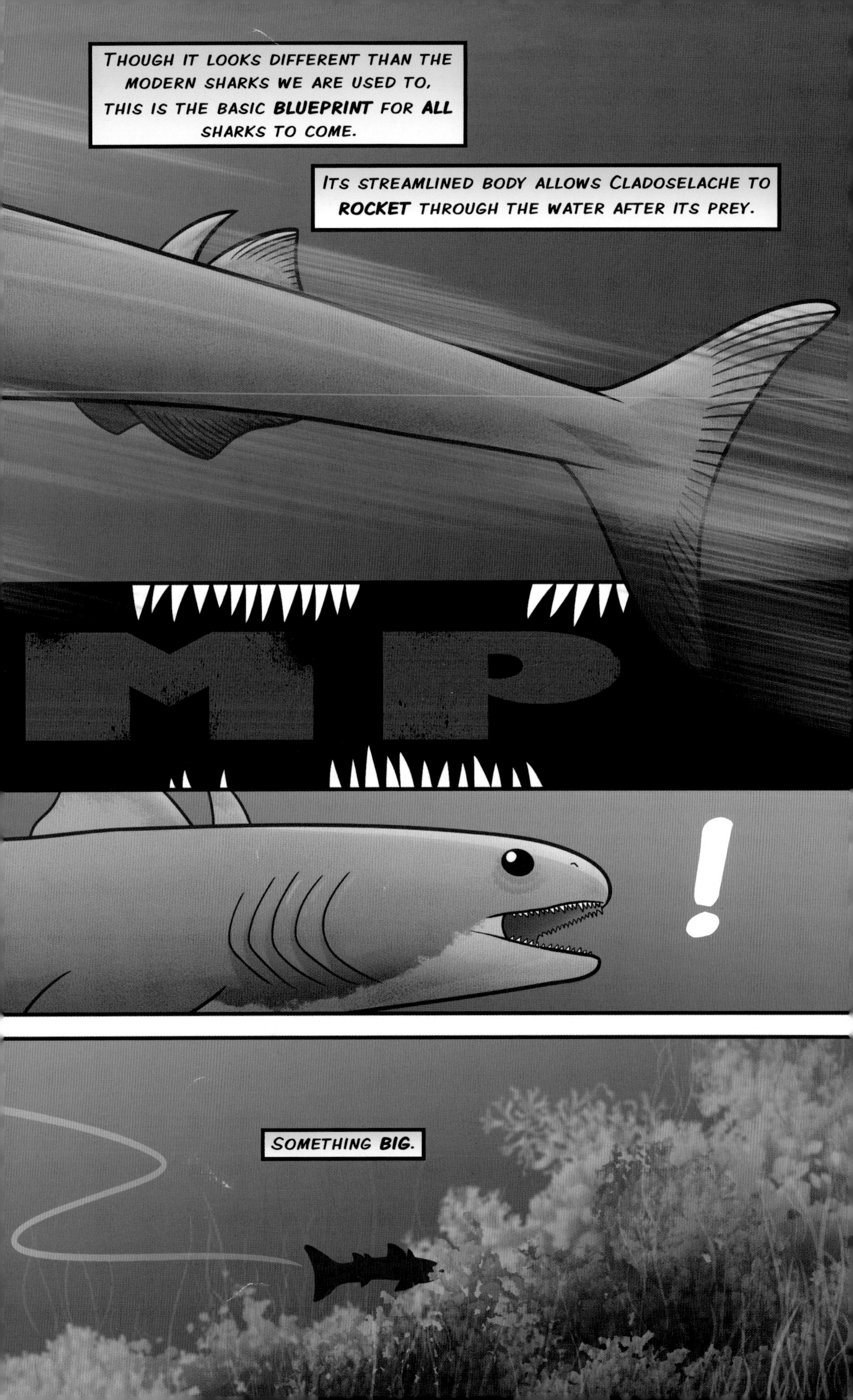
THOUGH IT LOOKS DIFFERENT THAN THE MODERN SHARKS WE ARE USED TO, THIS IS THE BASIC BLUEPRINT FOR ALL SHARKS TO COME.
ITS STREAMLINED BODY ALLOWS CLADOSELACHE TO ROCKET THROUGH THE WATER AFTER ITS PREY.
!
SOMETHING BIG.

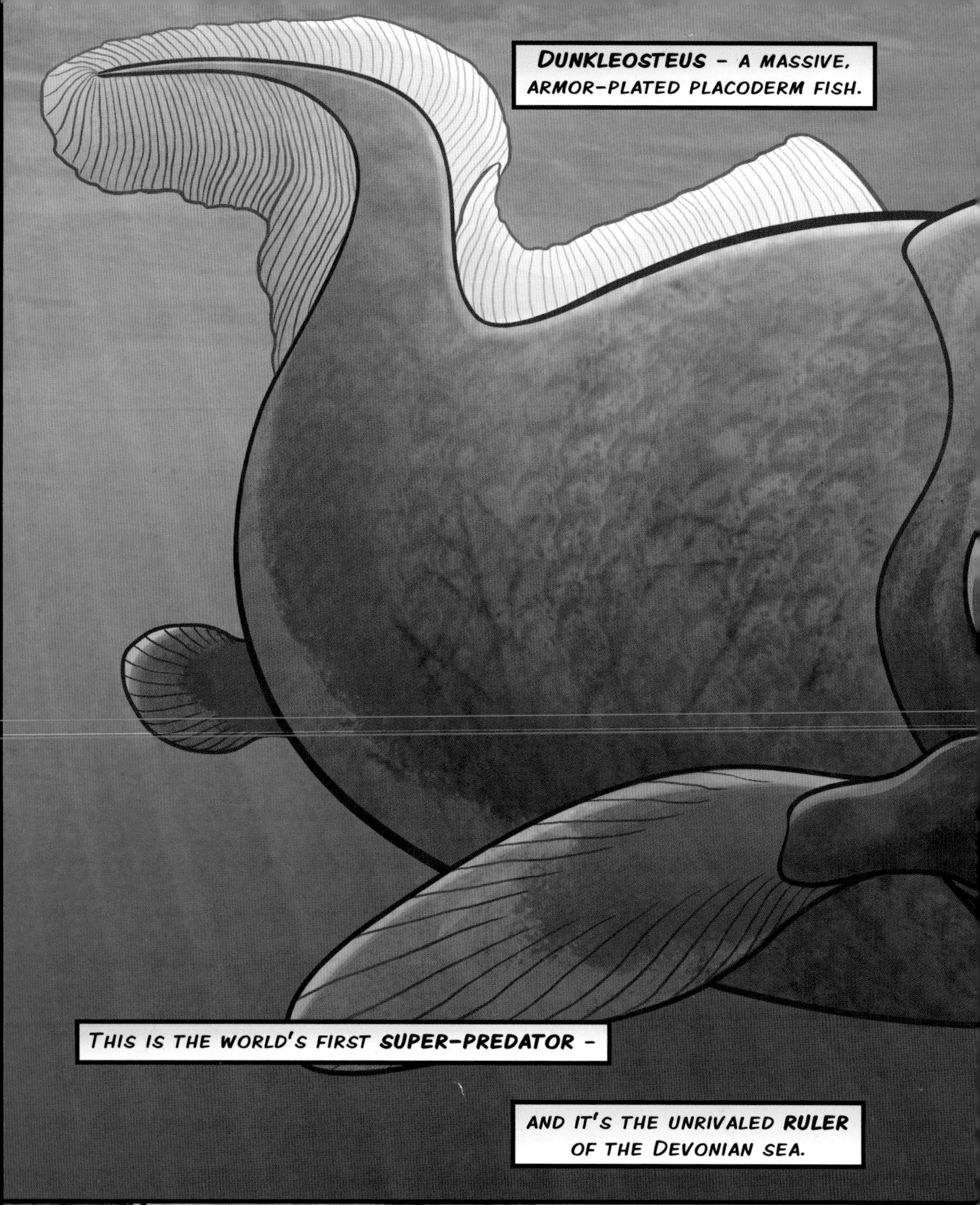
DUNKLEOSTEUS - A MASSIVE, ARMOR-PLATED PLACODERM FISH.
THIS IS THE WORLD'S FIRST SUPER-PREDATOR -
AND IT'S THE UNRIVALED RULER OF THE DEVONIAN SEA.

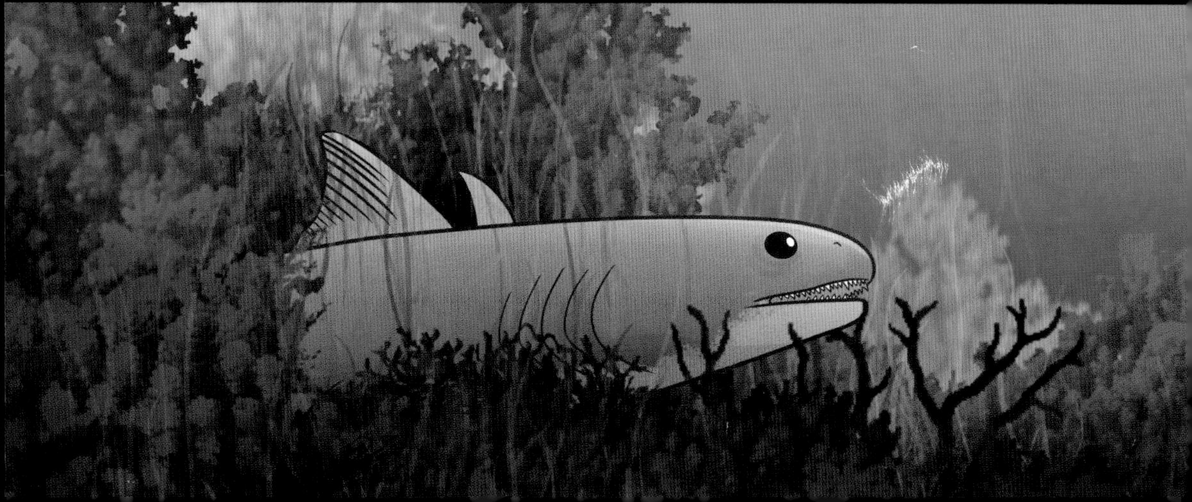

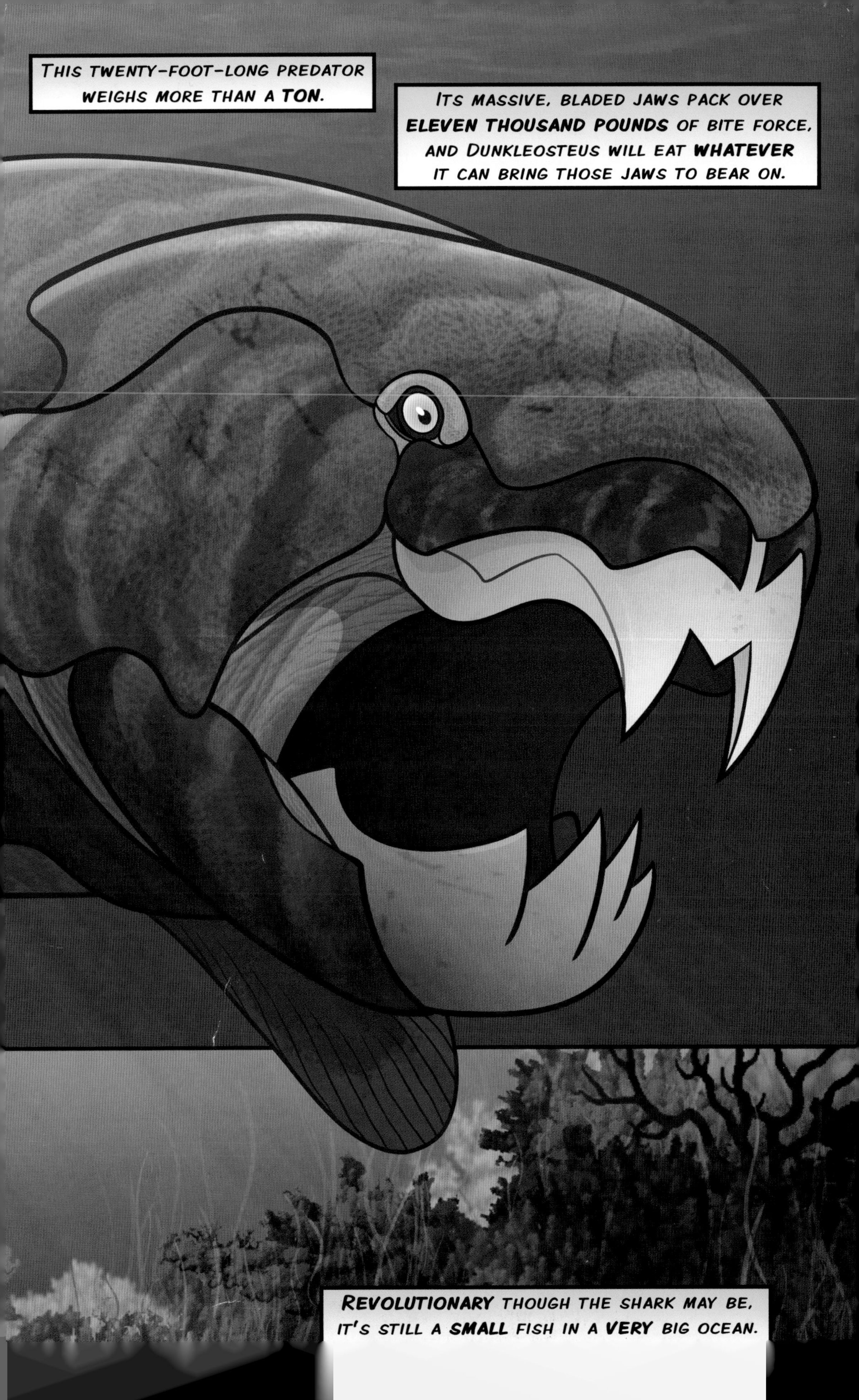
THIS TWENTY-FOOT-LONG PREDATOR WEIGHS MORE THAN A TON.
ITS MASSIVE, BLADED JAWS PACK OVER ELEVEN THOUSAND POUNDS OF BITE FORCE, AND DUNKLEOSTEUS WILL EAT WHATEVER IT CAN BRING THOSE JAWS TO BEAR ON.
REVOLUTIONARY THOUGH THE SHARK MAY BE, IT'S STILL A SMALL FISH IN A VERY BIG OCEAN.

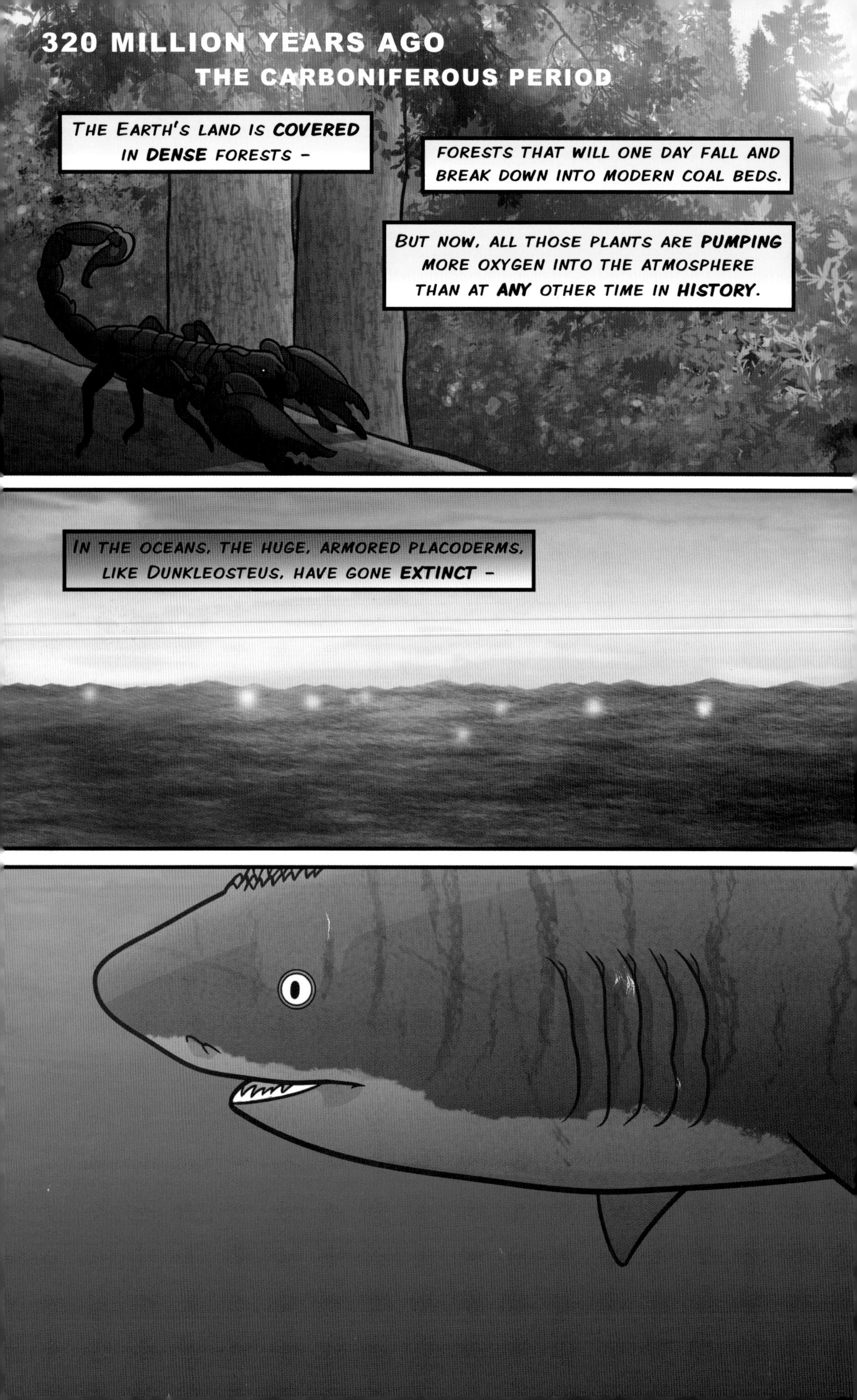
320 MILLION YEARS AGO
THE CARBONIFEROUS PERIOD
THE EARTH'S LAND IS COVERED IN DENSE FORESTS –
FORESTS THAT WILL ONE DAY FALL AND BREAK DOWN INTO MODERN COAL BEDS.
BUT NOW, ALL THOSE PLANTS ARE PUMPING MORE OXYGEN INTO THE ATMOSPHERE THAN AT ANY OTHER TIME IN HISTORY.
IN THE OCEANS, THE HUGE, ARMORED PLACODERMS, LIKE DUNKLEOSTEUS, HAVE GONE EXTINCT –

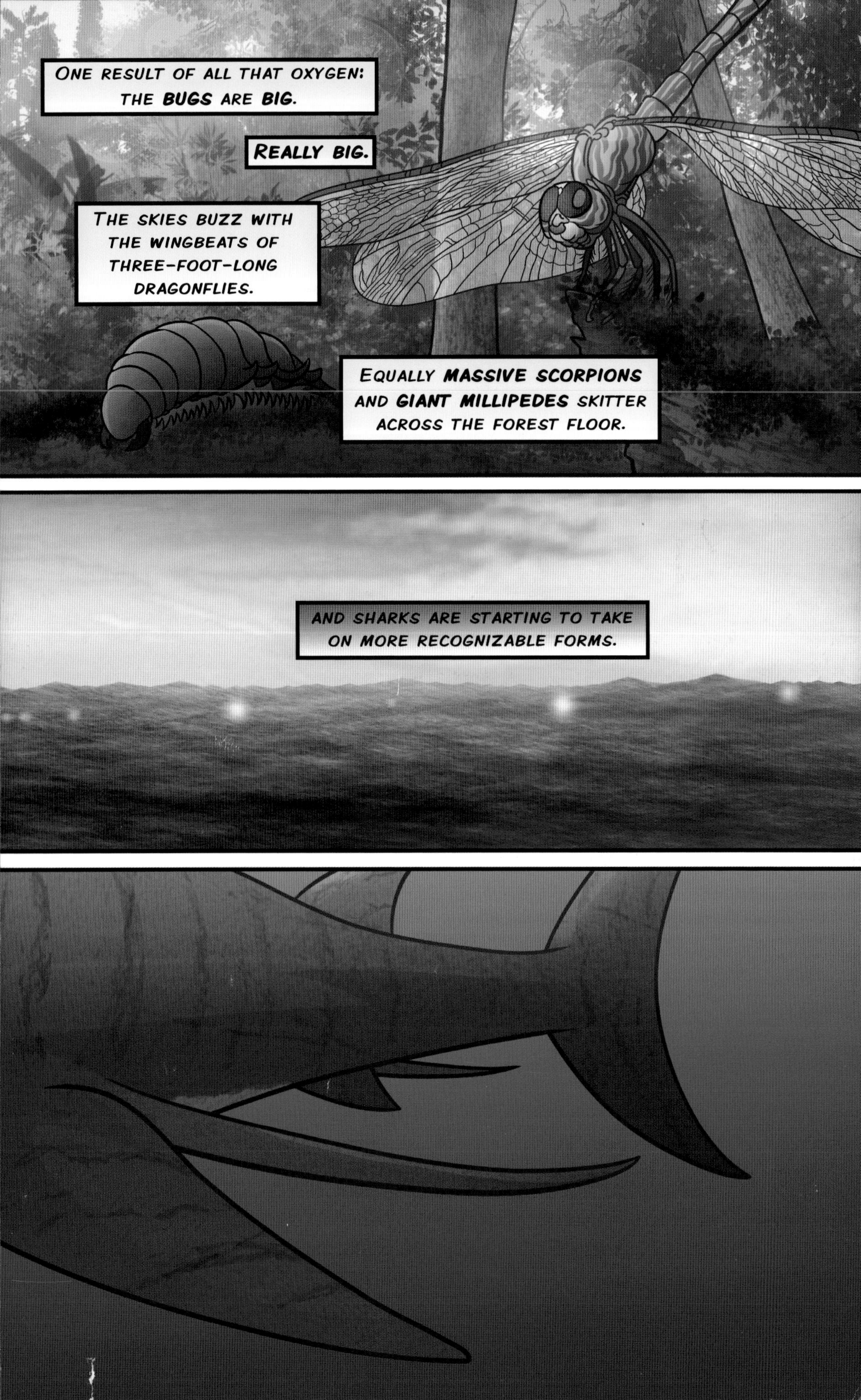
ONE RESULT OF ALL THAT OXYGEN: THE BUGS ARE BIG.
REALLY BIG.
THE SKIES BUZZ WITH THE WINGBEATS OF THREE-FOOT-LONG DRAGONFLIES.
EQUALLY MASSIVE SCORPIONS AND GIANT MILLIPEDES SKITTER ACROSS THE FOREST FLOOR.
AND SHARKS ARE STARTING TO TAKE ON MORE RECOGNIZABLE FORMS.

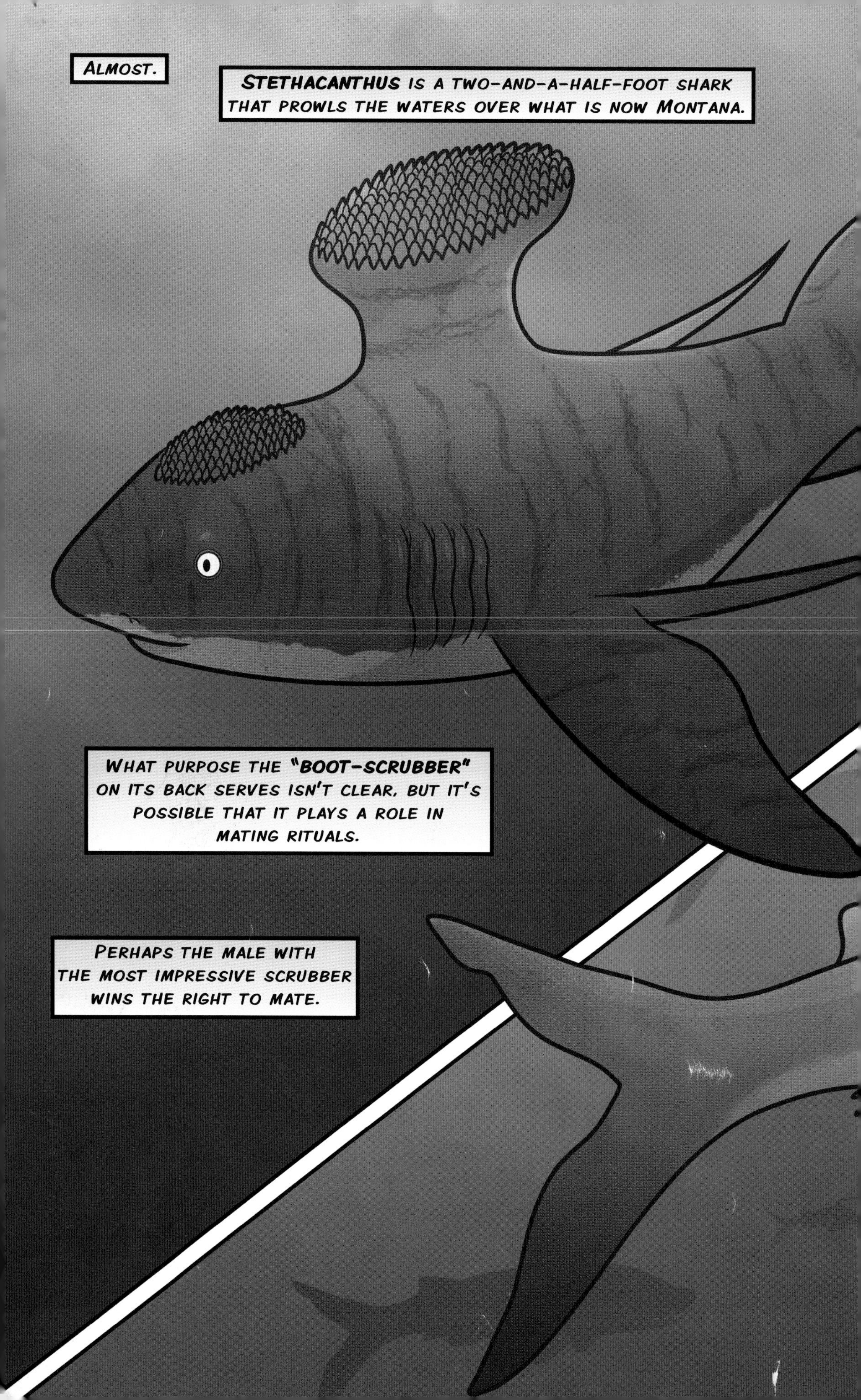
Almost.
Stethacanthus is a two-and-a-half-foot shark that prowls the waters over what is now Montana.
What purpose the "boot-scrubber" on its back serves isn't clear, but it's possible that it plays a role in mating rituals.
Perhaps the male with the most impressive scrubber wins the right to mate.

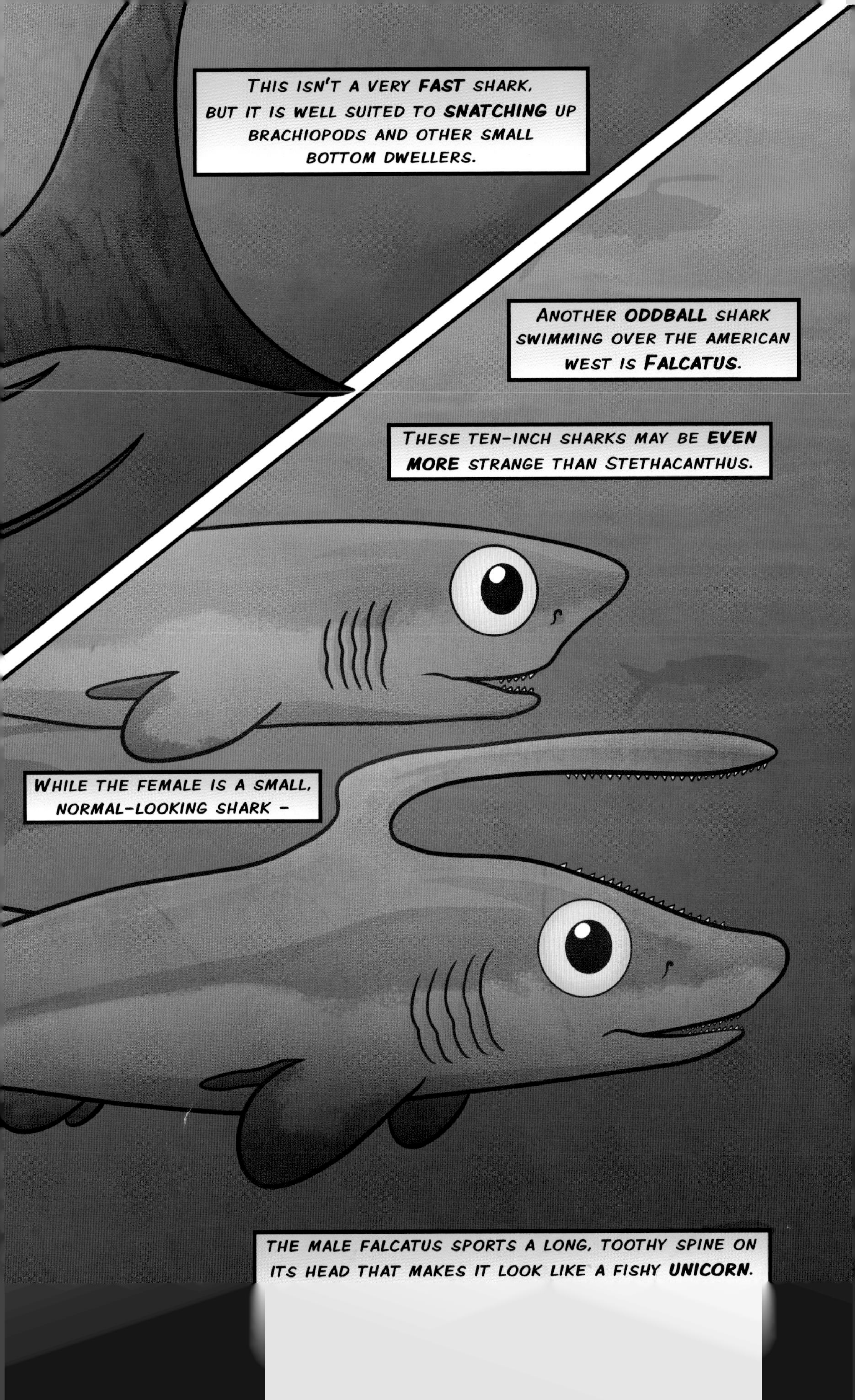
THIS ISN'T A VERY FAST SHARK, BUT IT IS WELL SUITED TO SNATCHING UP BRACHIOPODS AND OTHER SMALL BOTTOM DWELLERS.
ANOTHER ODDBALL SHARK SWIMMING OVER THE AMERICAN WEST IS FALCATUS.
THESE TEN-INCH SHARKS MAY BE EVEN MORE STRANGE THAN STETHACANTHUS.
WHILE THE FEMALE IS A SMALL, NORMAL-LOOKING SHARK –
THE MALE FALCATUS SPORTS A LONG, TOOTHY SPINE ON ITS HEAD THAT MAKES IT LOOK LIKE A FISHY UNICORN.

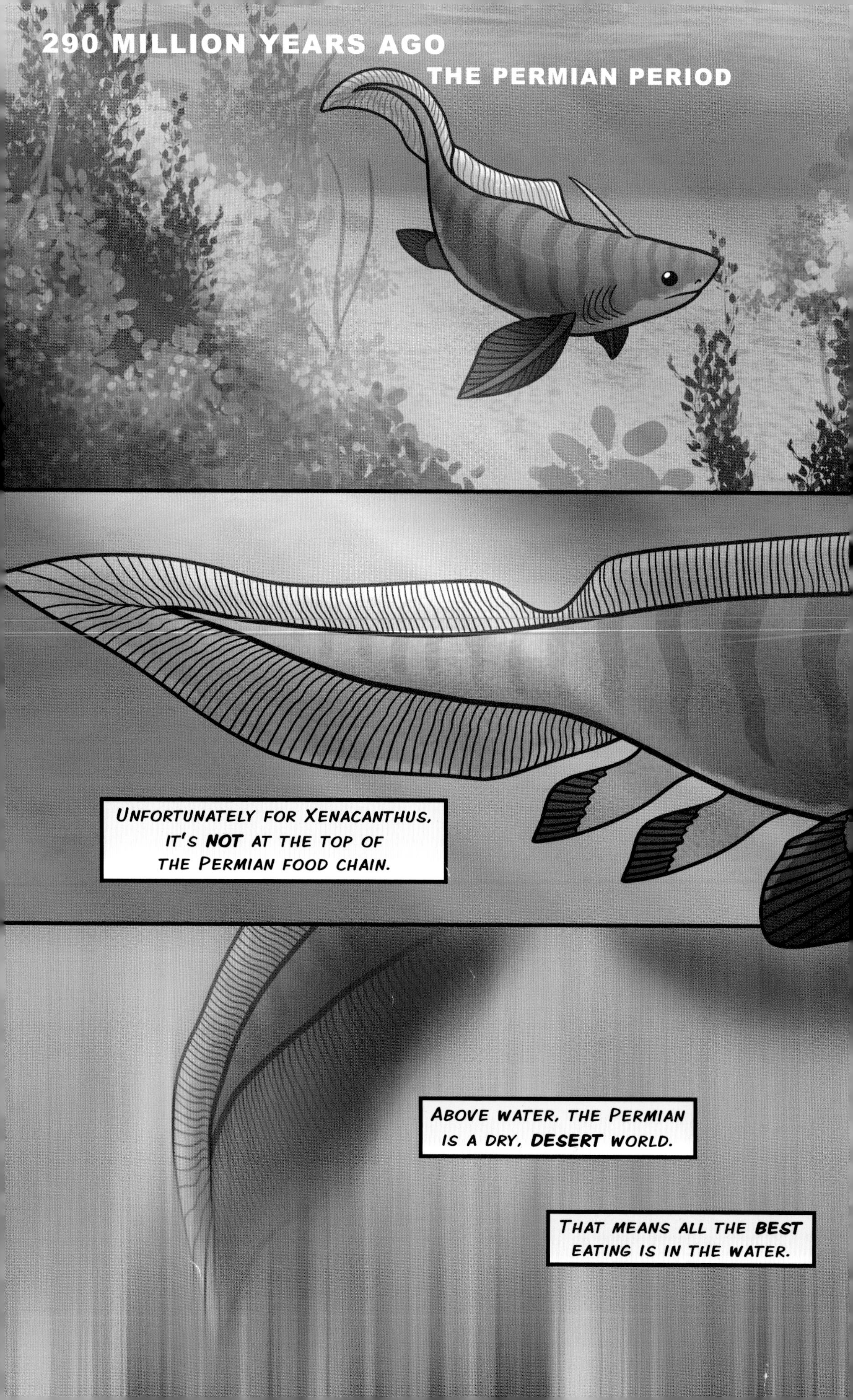
290 MILLION YEARS AGO
THE PERMIAN PERIOD
UNFORTUNATELY FOR XENACANTHUS, IT'S **NOT** AT THE TOP OF THE PERMIAN FOOD CHAIN.
ABOVE WATER, THE PERMIAN IS A DRY, **DESERT** WORLD.
THAT MEANS ALL THE **BEST** EATING IS IN THE WATER.

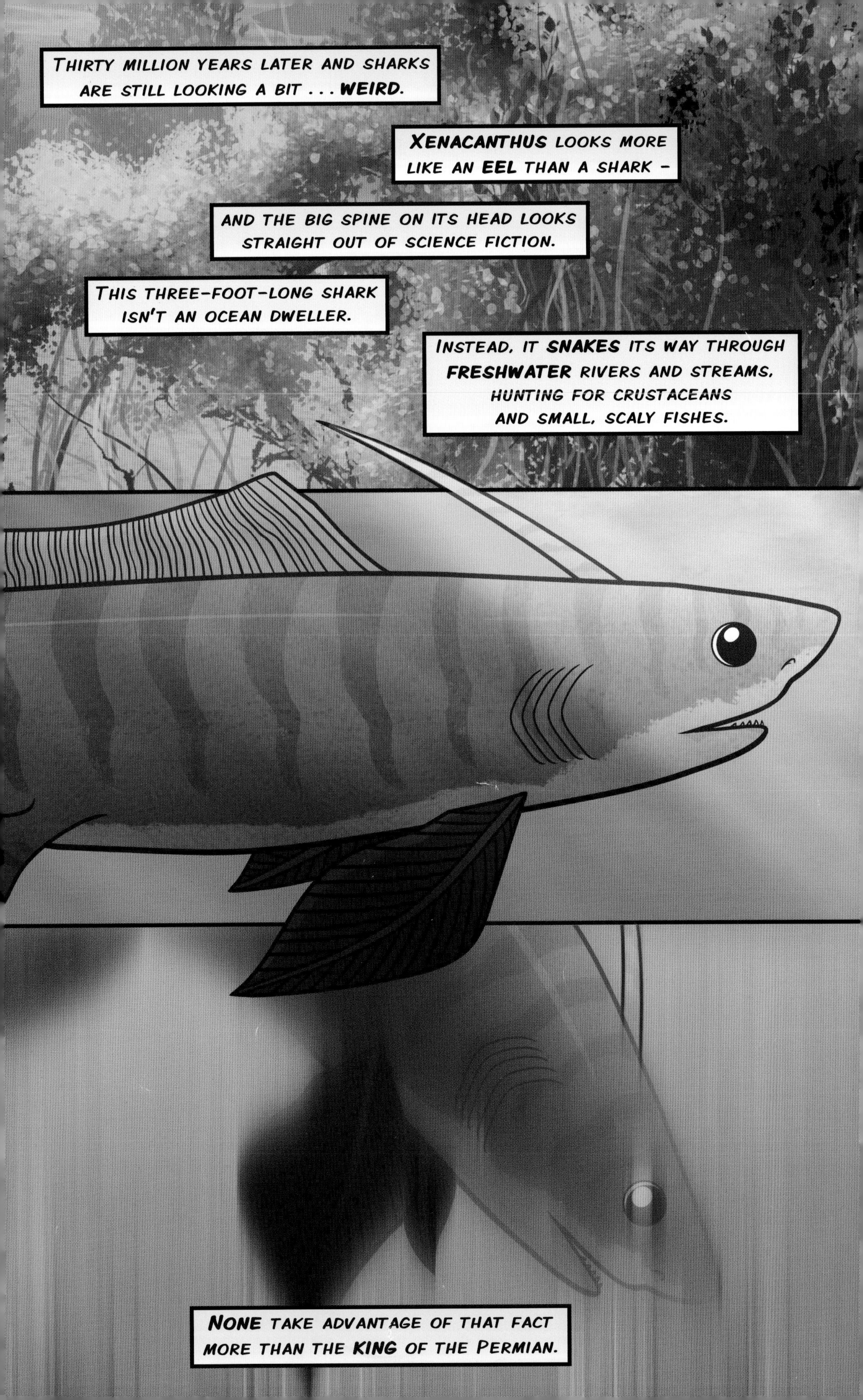
THIRTY MILLION YEARS LATER AND SHARKS ARE STILL LOOKING A BIT . . . WEIRD.
XENACANTHUS LOOKS MORE LIKE AN EEL THAN A SHARK –
AND THE BIG SPINE ON ITS HEAD LOOKS STRAIGHT OUT OF SCIENCE FICTION.
THIS THREE-FOOT-LONG SHARK ISN'T AN OCEAN DWELLER.
INSTEAD, IT SNAKES ITS WAY THROUGH FRESHWATER RIVERS AND STREAMS, HUNTING FOR CRUSTACEANS AND SMALL, SCALY FISHES.
NONE TAKE ADVANTAGE OF THAT FACT MORE THAN THE KING OF THE PERMIAN.

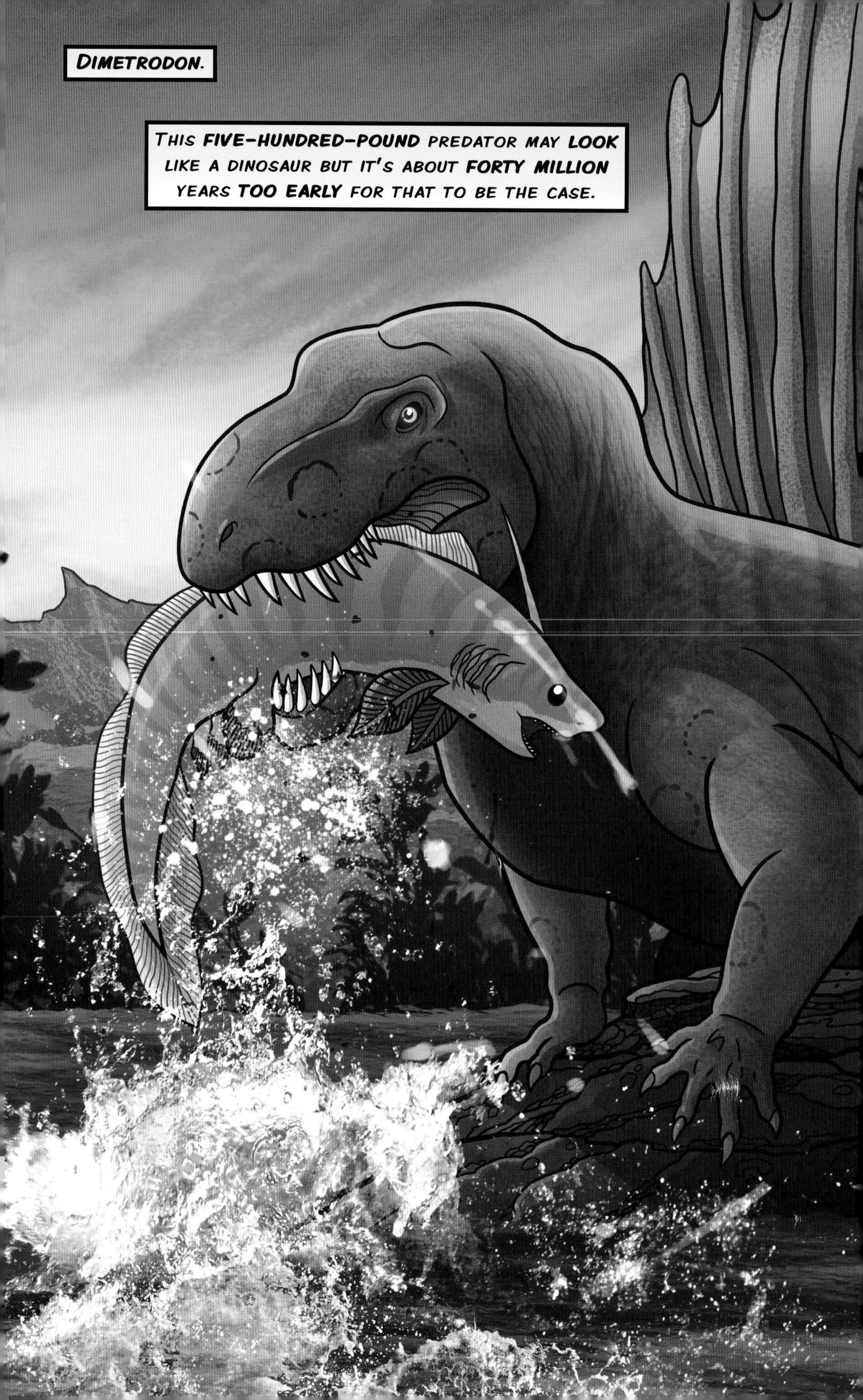
DIMETRODON.
THIS FIVE-HUNDRED-POUND PREDATOR MAY LOOK LIKE A DINOSAUR BUT IT'S ABOUT FORTY MILLION YEARS TOO EARLY FOR THAT TO BE THE CASE.

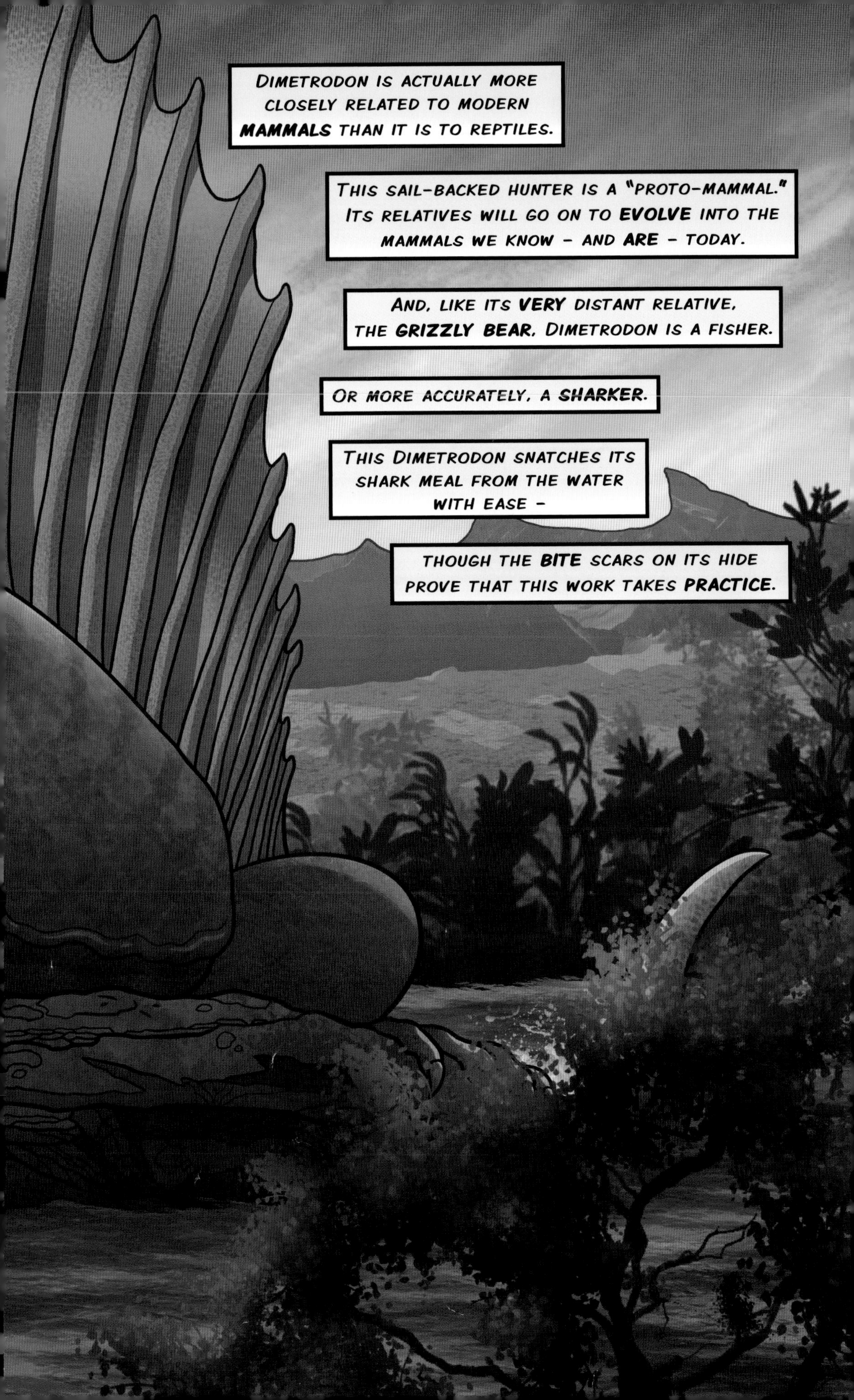
DIMETRODON IS ACTUALLY MORE CLOSELY RELATED TO MODERN MAMMALS THAN IT IS TO REPTILES.
THIS SAIL-BACKED HUNTER IS A "PROTO-MAMMAL." ITS RELATIVES WILL GO ON TO EVOLVE INTO THE MAMMALS WE KNOW - AND ARE - TODAY.
AND, LIKE ITS VERY DISTANT RELATIVE, THE GRIZZLY BEAR, DIMETRODON IS A FISHER.
OR MORE ACCURATELY, A SHARKER.
THIS DIMETRODON SNATCHES ITS SHARK MEAL FROM THE WATER WITH EASE -
THOUGH THE BITE SCARS ON ITS HIDE PROVE THAT THIS WORK TAKES PRACTICE.

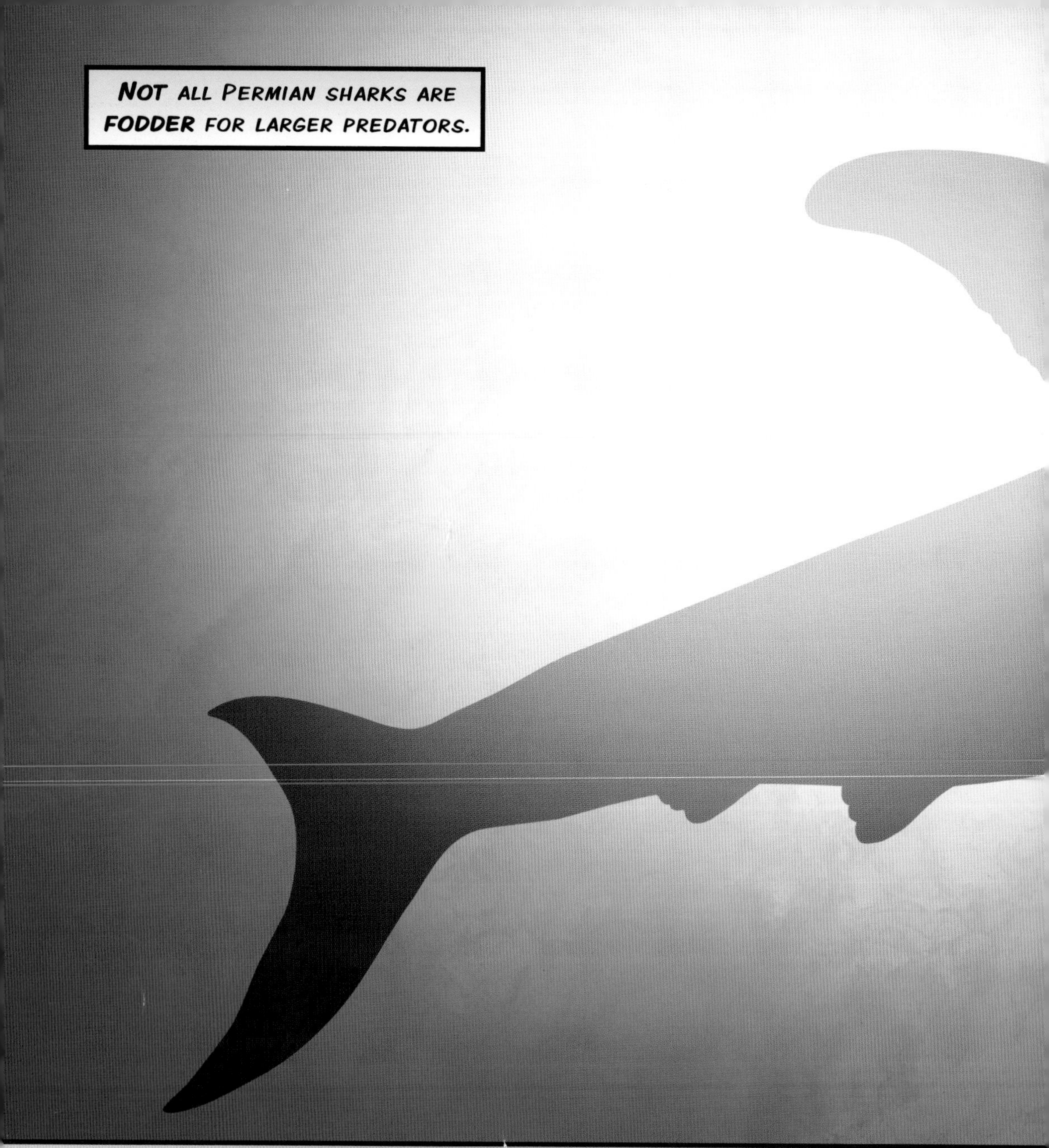
NOT ALL PERMIAN SHARKS ARE FODDER FOR LARGER PREDATORS.
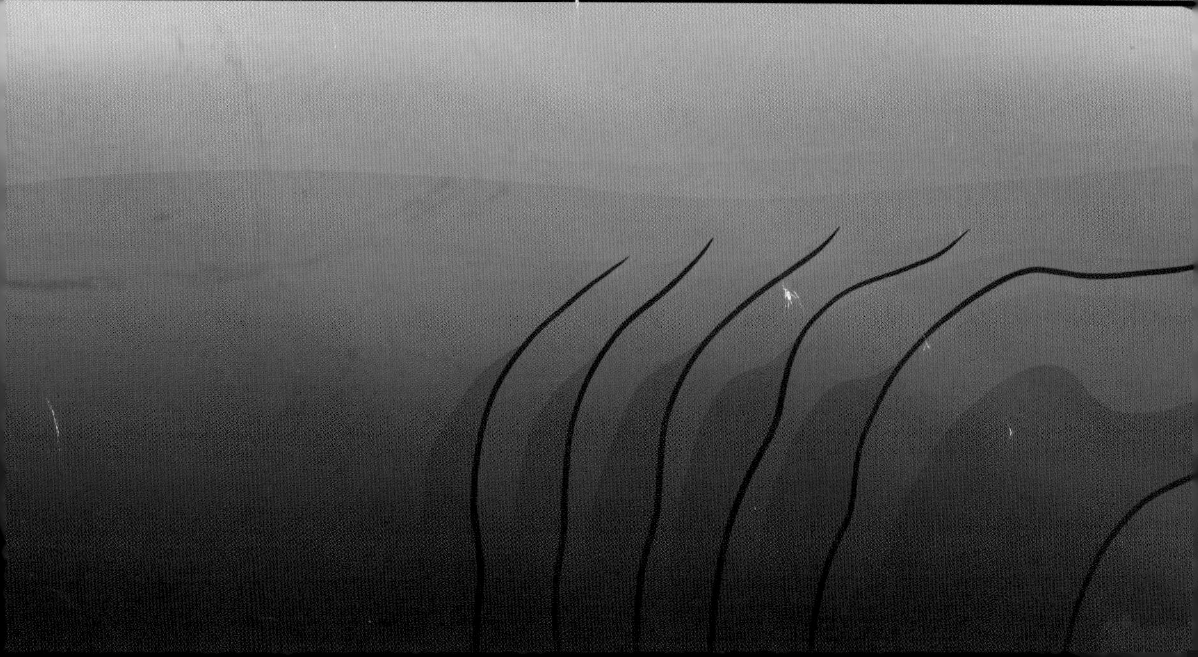

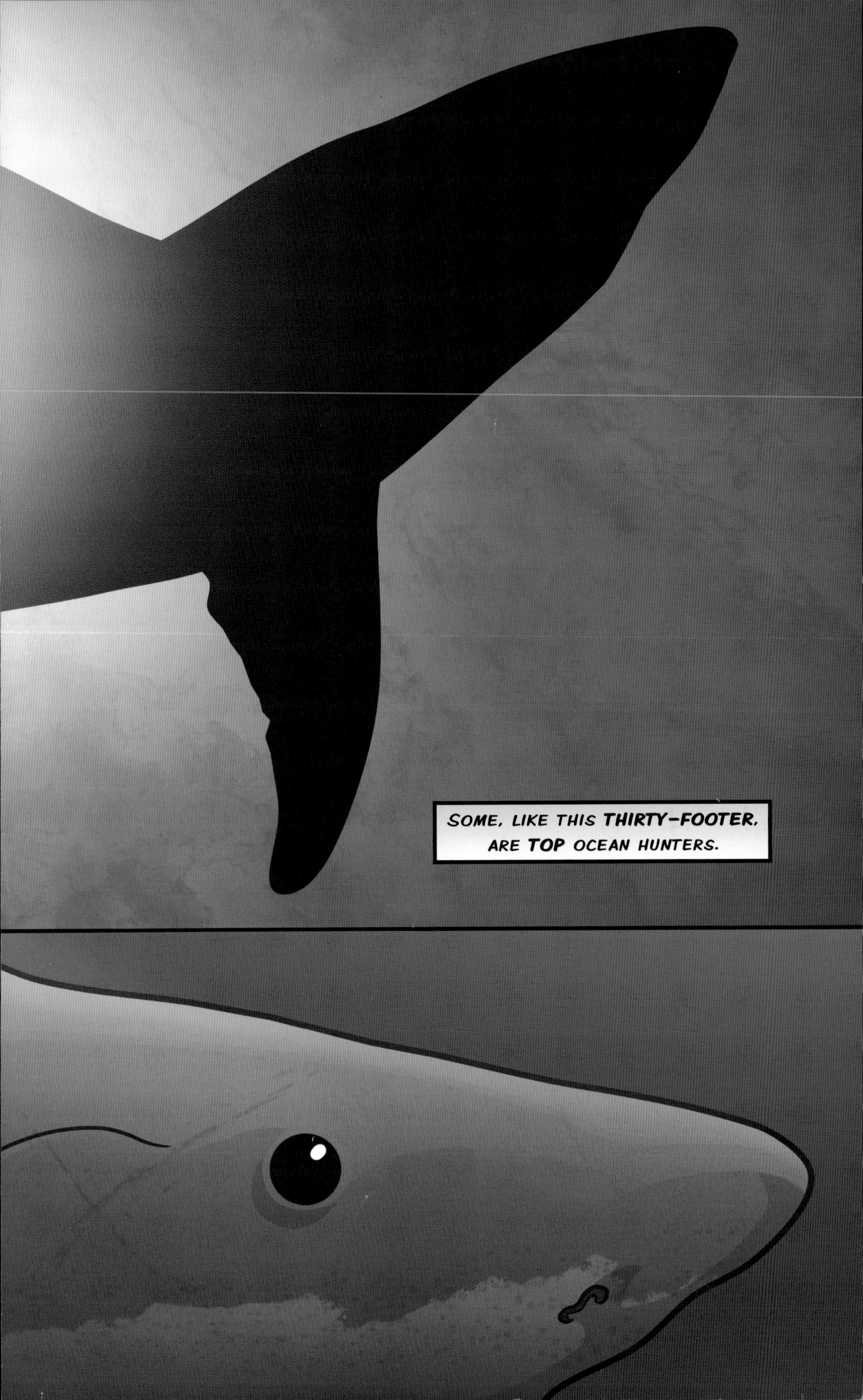
SOME, LIKE THIS THIRTY-FOOTER, ARE TOP OCEAN HUNTERS.

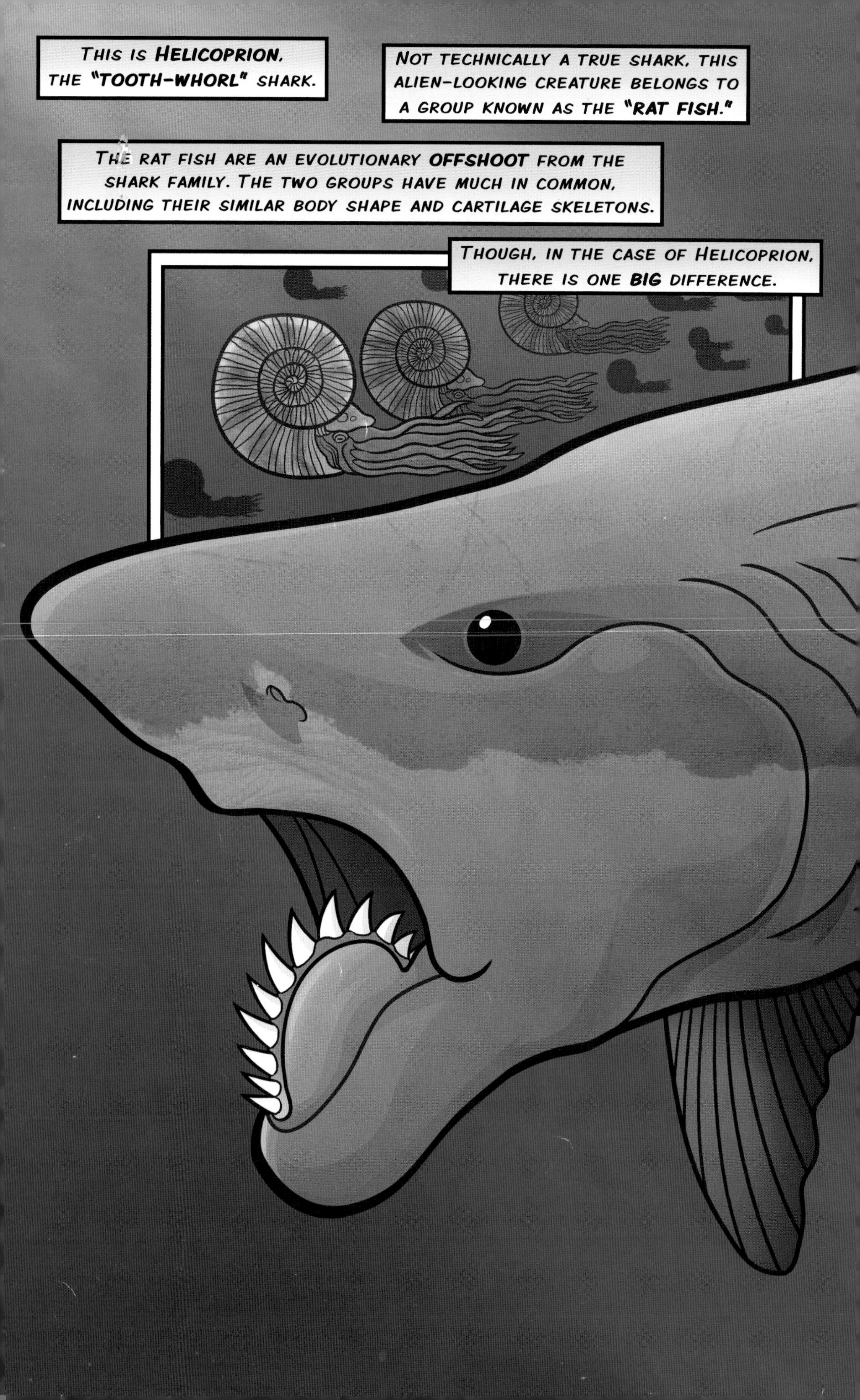
THIS IS HELICOPRION, THE "TOOTH-WHORL" SHARK.
NOT TECHNICALLY A TRUE SHARK, THIS ALIEN-LOOKING CREATURE BELONGS TO A GROUP KNOWN AS THE "RAT FISH."
THE RAT FISH ARE AN EVOLUTIONARY OFFSHOOT FROM THE SHARK FAMILY. THE TWO GROUPS HAVE MUCH IN COMMON, INCLUDING THEIR SIMILAR BODY SHAPE AND CARTILAGE SKELETONS.
THOUGH, IN THE CASE OF HELICOPRION, THERE IS ONE BIG DIFFERENCE.

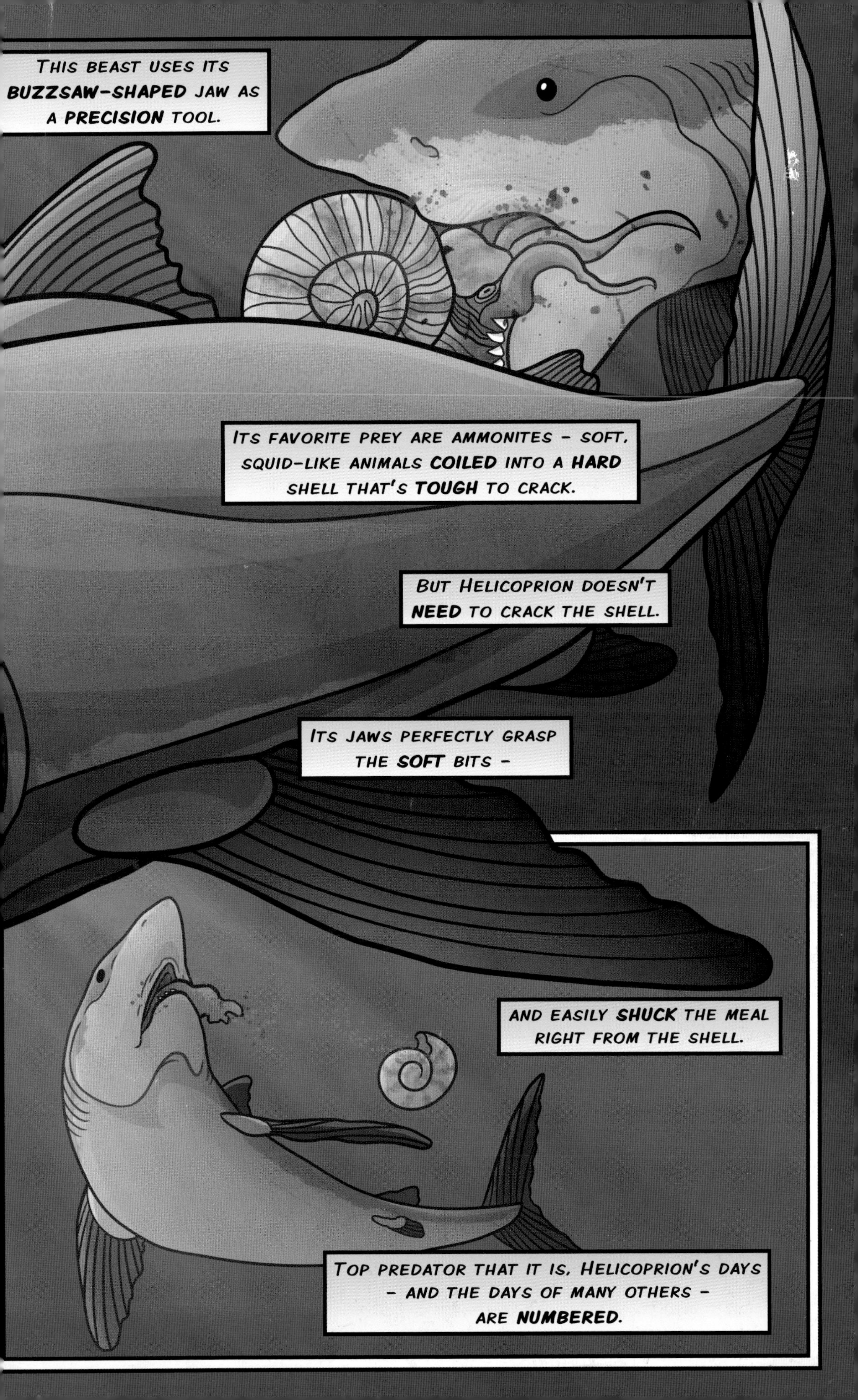
THIS BEAST USES ITS **BUZZSAW-SHAPED** JAW AS A **PRECISION** TOOL.
ITS FAVORITE PREY ARE AMMONITES – SOFT, SQUID-LIKE ANIMALS **COILED** INTO A **HARD** SHELL THAT'S **TOUGH** TO CRACK.
BUT HELICOPRION DOESN'T **NEED** TO CRACK THE SHELL.
ITS JAWS PERFECTLY GRASP THE **SOFT** BITS –
AND EASILY **SHUCK** THE MEAL RIGHT FROM THE SHELL.
TOP PREDATOR THAT IT IS, HELICOPRION'S DAYS – AND THE DAYS OF MANY OTHERS – ARE **NUMBERED**.

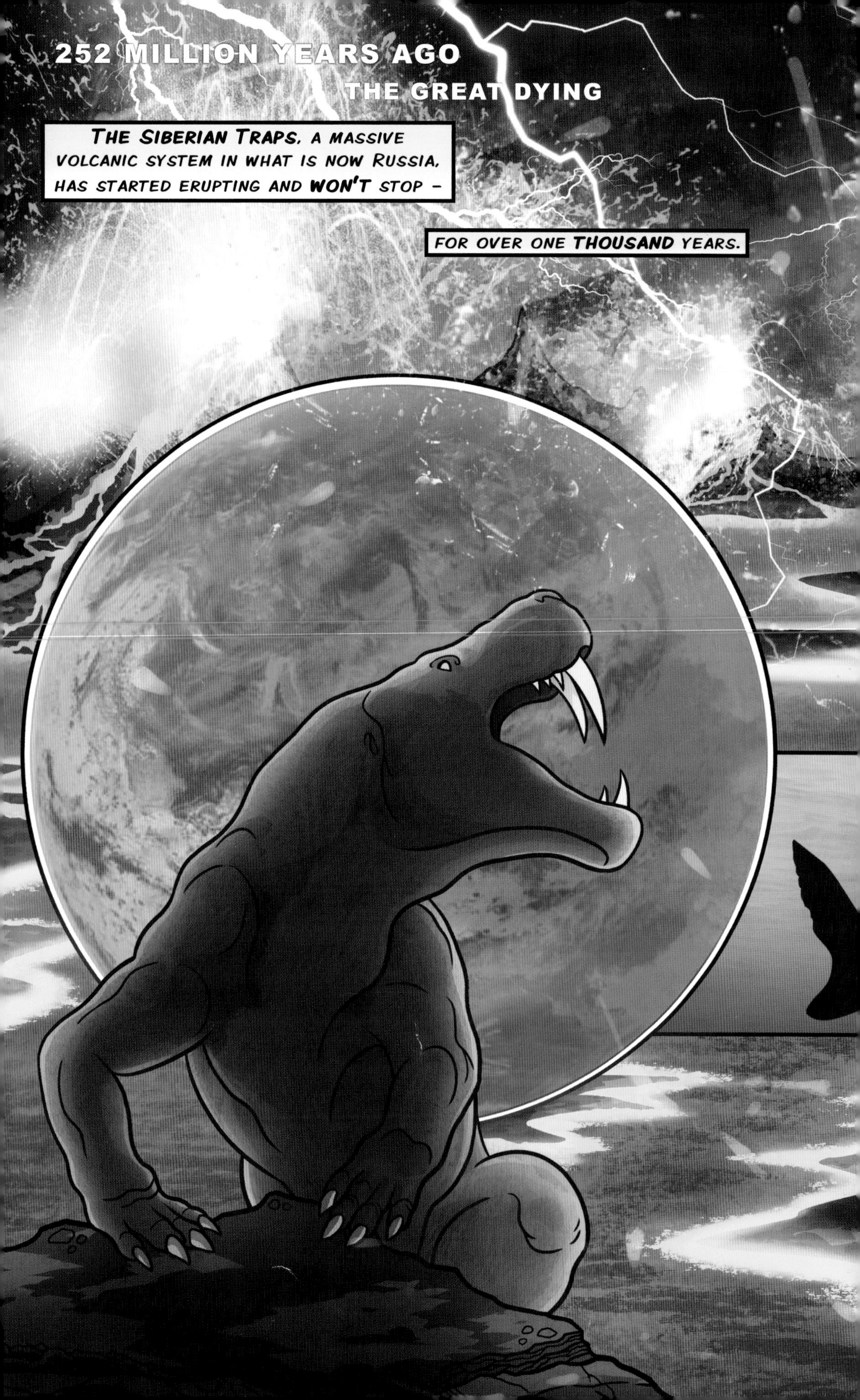
252 MILLION YEARS AGO
THE GREAT DYING
THE SIBERIAN TRAPS, A MASSIVE VOLCANIC SYSTEM IN WHAT IS NOW RUSSIA, HAS STARTED ERUPTING AND WON'T STOP –
FOR OVER ONE THOUSAND YEARS.

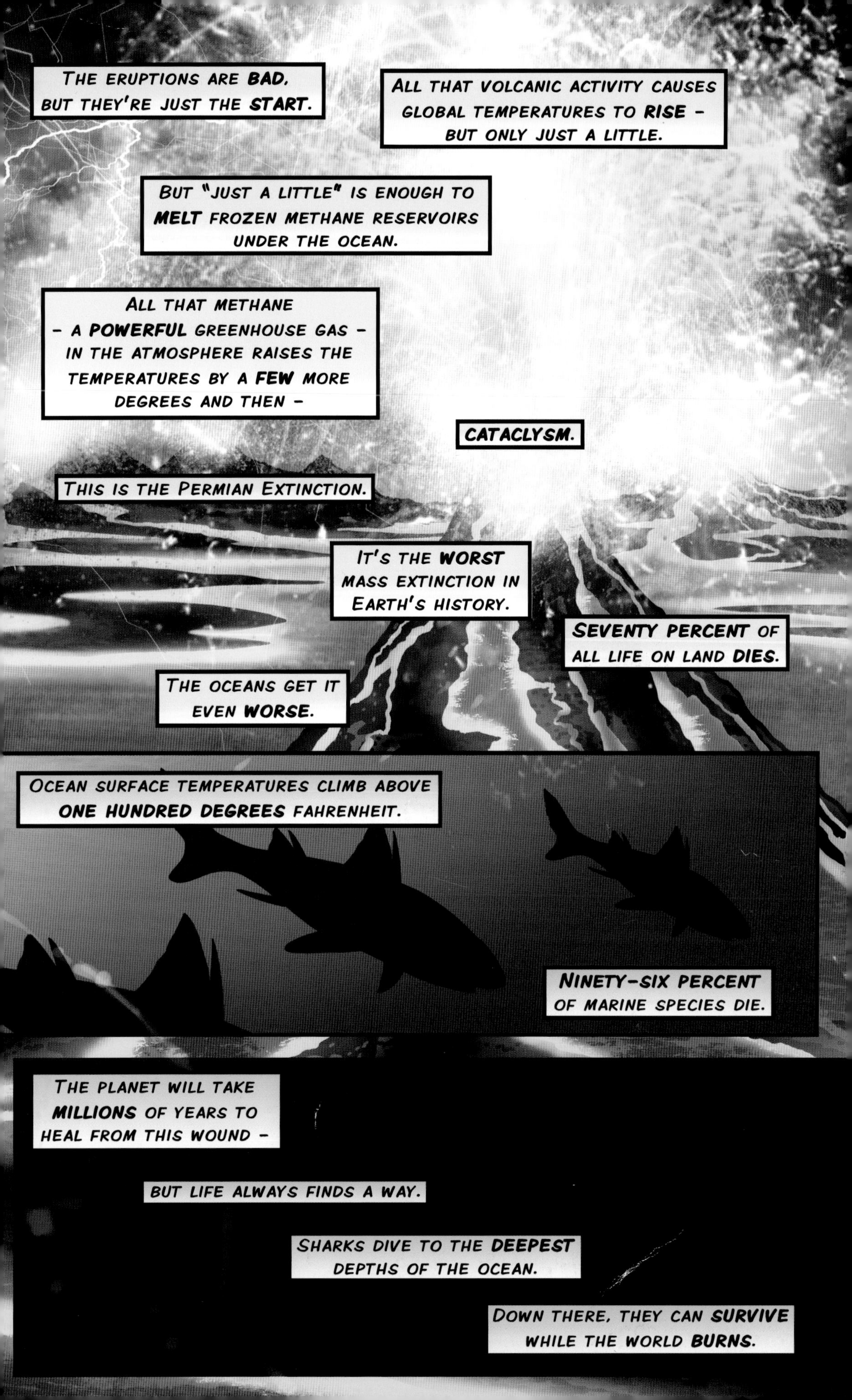

The eruptions are bad, but they're just the start.
All that volcanic activity causes global temperatures to rise – but only just a little.
But "just a little" is enough to melt frozen methane reservoirs under the ocean.
All that methane – a powerful greenhouse gas – in the atmosphere raises the temperatures by a few more degrees and then –
Cataclysm.
This is the Permian Extinction.
It's the worst mass extinction in Earth's history.
Seventy percent of all life on land dies.
The oceans get it even worse.
Ocean surface temperatures climb above one hundred degrees Fahrenheit.
Ninety-six percent of marine species die.
The planet will take millions of years to heal from this wound –
but life always finds a way.
Sharks dive to the deepest depths of the ocean.
Down there, they can survive while the world burns.

PART TWO

MESOZOIC

<u>252 - 66</u>
MILLION YEARS AGO

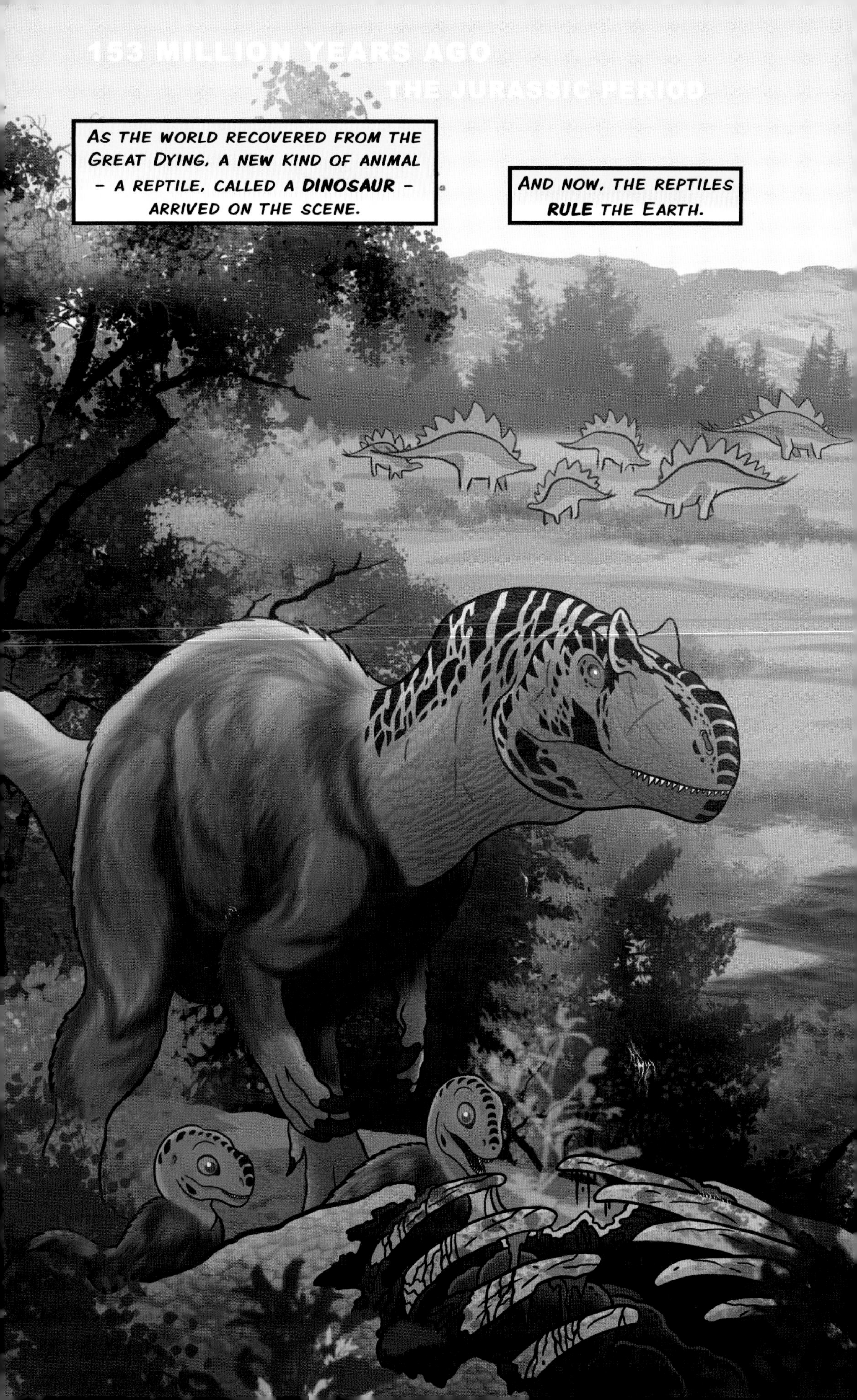
153 MILLION YEARS AGO
THE JURASSIC PERIOD
AS THE WORLD RECOVERED FROM THE GREAT DYING, A NEW KIND OF ANIMAL - A REPTILE, CALLED A DINOSAUR - ARRIVED ON THE SCENE.
AND NOW, THE REPTILES RULE THE EARTH.

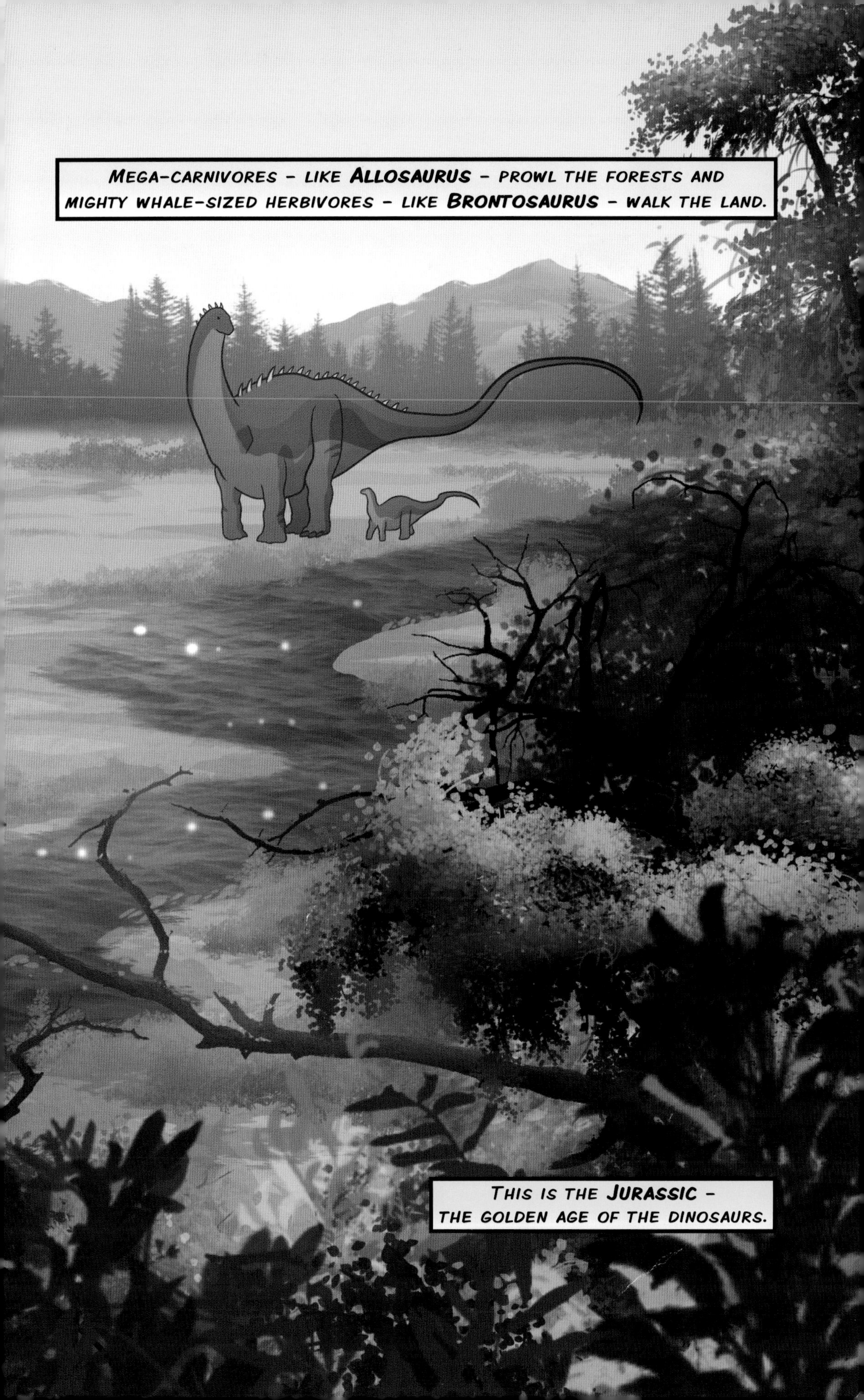
MEGA-CARNIVORES - LIKE ALLOSAURUS - PROWL THE FORESTS AND MIGHTY WHALE-SIZED HERBIVORES - LIKE BRONTOSAURUS - WALK THE LAND.
THIS IS THE JURASSIC - THE GOLDEN AGE OF THE DINOSAURS.

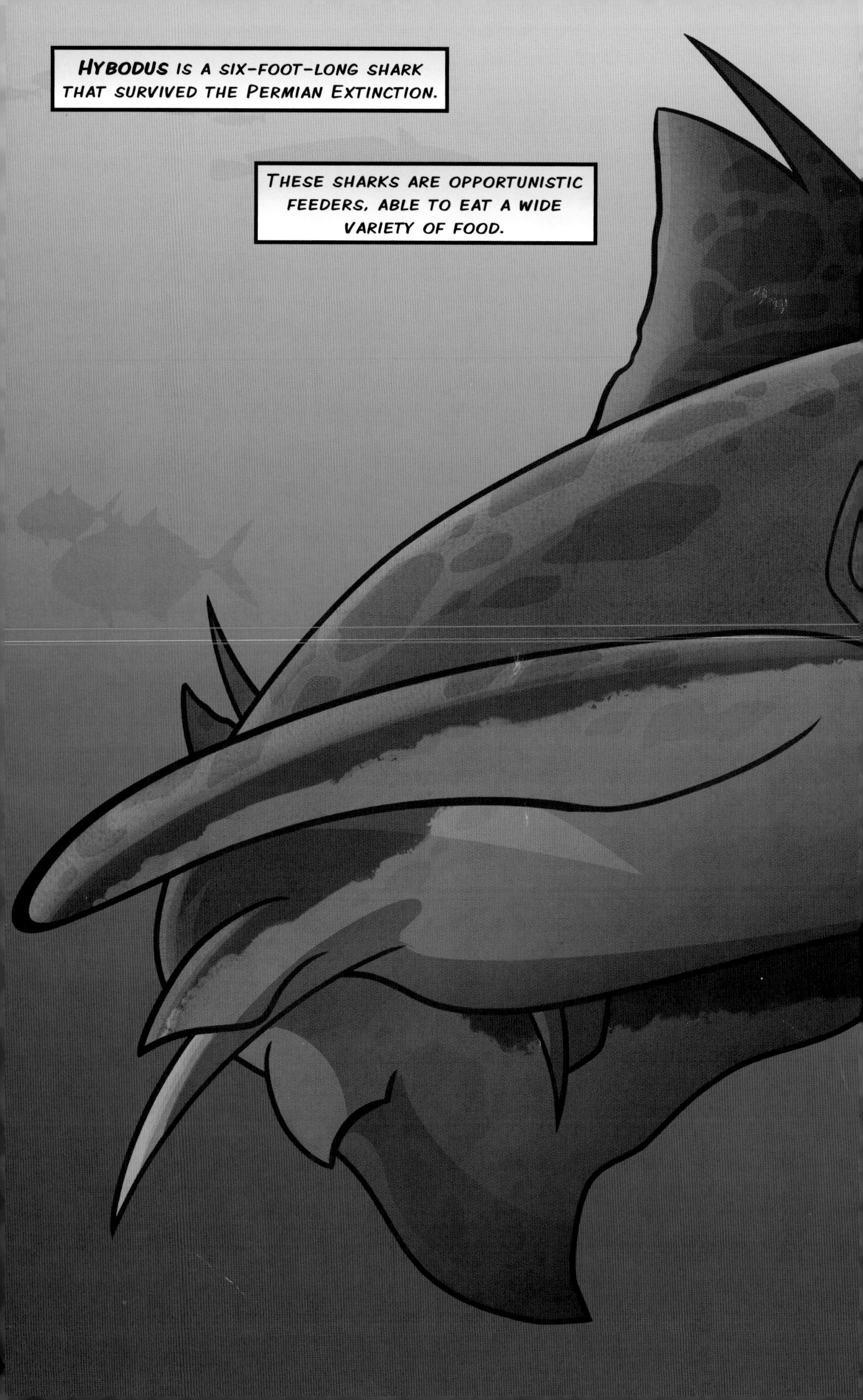
HYBODUS IS A SIX-FOOT-LONG SHARK THAT SURVIVED THE PERMIAN EXTINCTION.
THESE SHARKS ARE OPPORTUNISTIC FEEDERS, ABLE TO EAT A WIDE VARIETY OF FOOD.

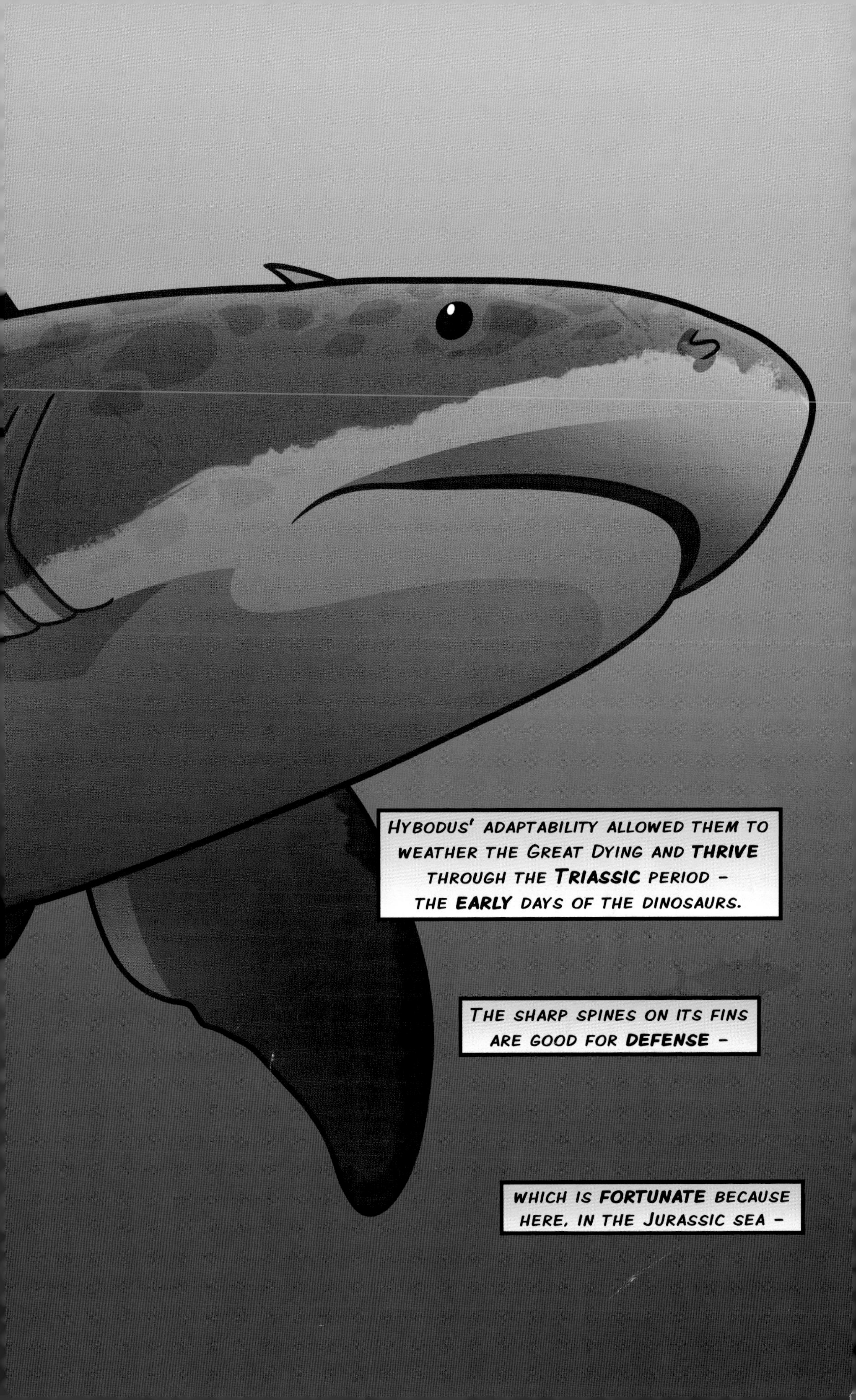
HYBODUS' ADAPTABILITY ALLOWED THEM TO WEATHER THE GREAT DYING AND THRIVE THROUGH THE TRIASSIC PERIOD – THE EARLY DAYS OF THE DINOSAURS.
THE SHARP SPINES ON ITS FINS ARE GOOD FOR DEFENSE –
WHICH IS FORTUNATE BECAUSE HERE, IN THE JURASSIC SEA –

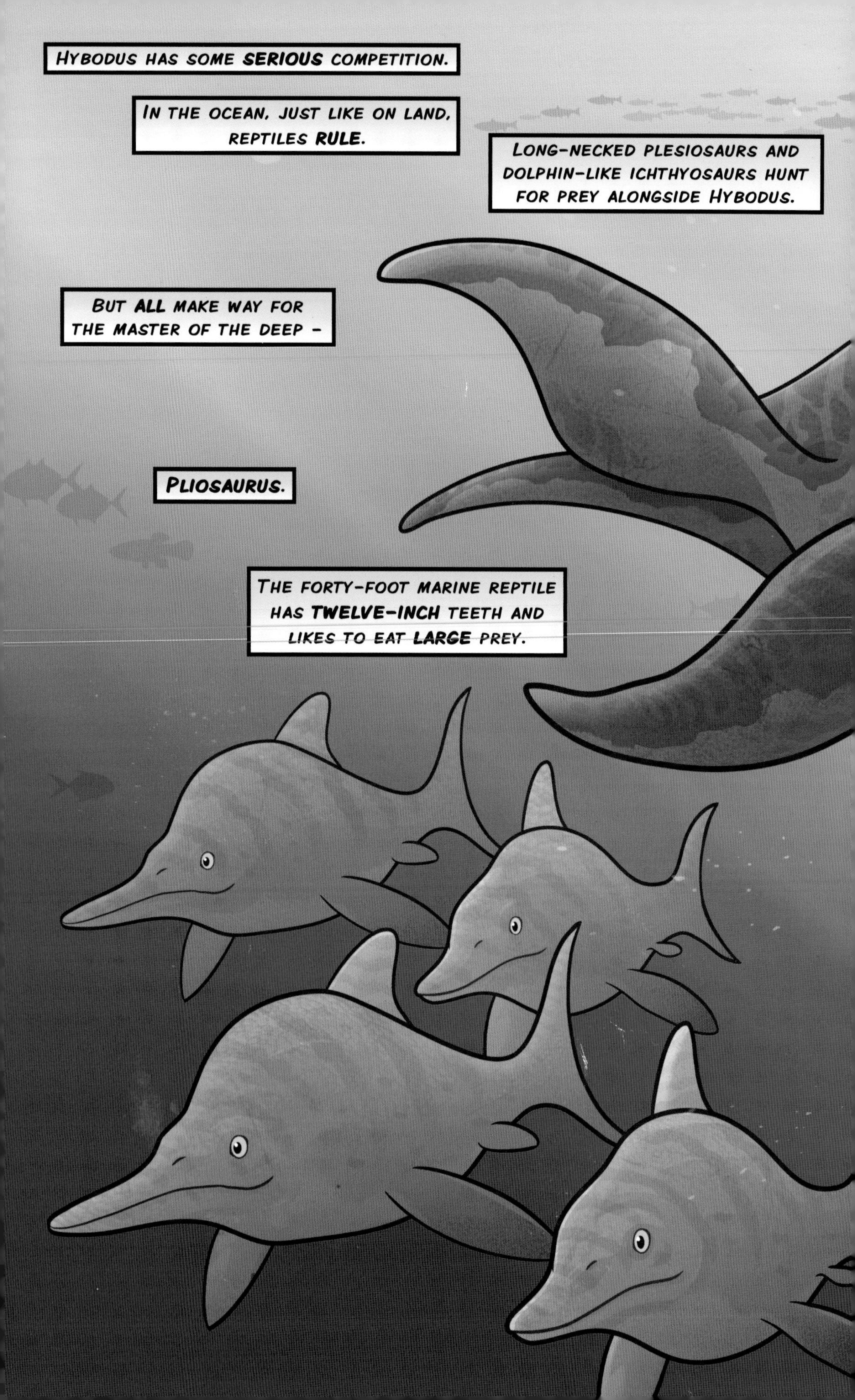
HYBODUS HAS SOME SERIOUS COMPETITION.
IN THE OCEAN, JUST LIKE ON LAND, REPTILES RULE.
LONG-NECKED PLESIOSAURS AND DOLPHIN-LIKE ICHTHYOSAURS HUNT FOR PREY ALONGSIDE HYBODUS.
BUT ALL MAKE WAY FOR THE MASTER OF THE DEEP –
PLIOSAURUS.
THE FORTY-FOOT MARINE REPTILE HAS TWELVE-INCH TEETH AND LIKES TO EAT LARGE PREY.

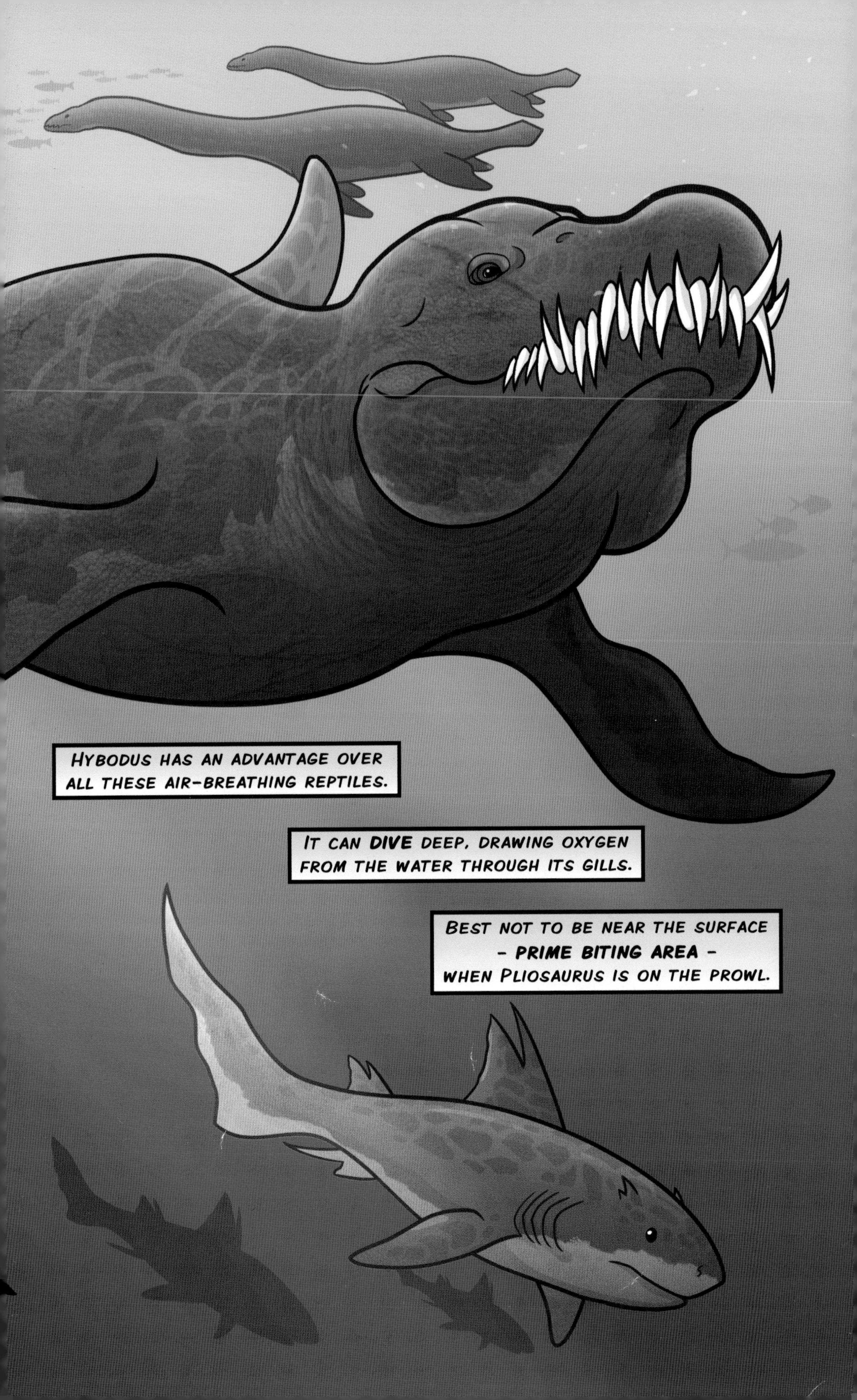
HYBODUS HAS AN ADVANTAGE OVER ALL THESE AIR-BREATHING REPTILES.
IT CAN **DIVE** DEEP, DRAWING OXYGEN FROM THE WATER THROUGH ITS GILLS.
BEST NOT TO BE NEAR THE SURFACE - **PRIME BITING AREA** - WHEN PLIOSAURUS IS ON THE PROWL.

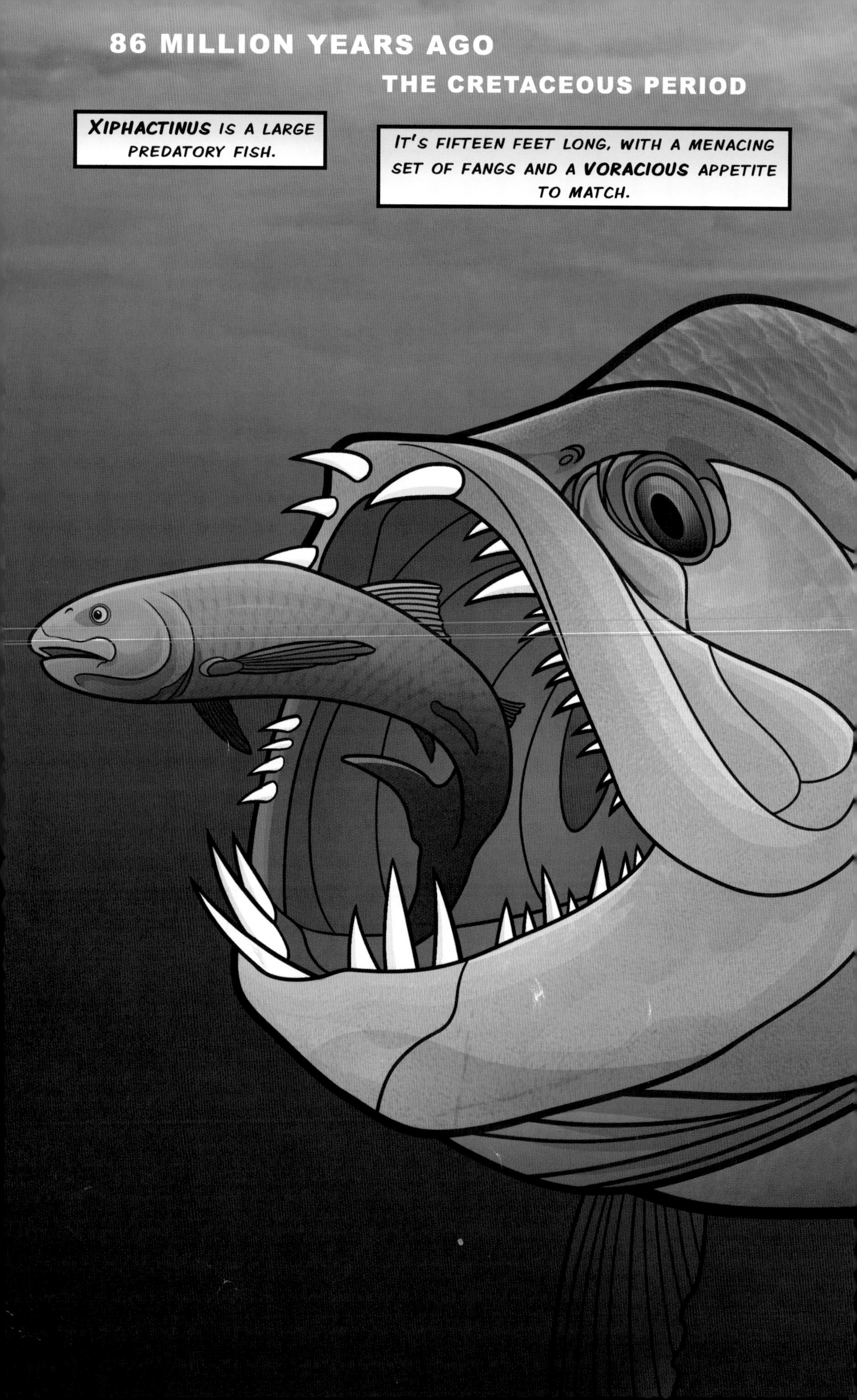
86 MILLION YEARS AGO
THE CRETACEOUS PERIOD
XIPHACTINUS IS A LARGE PREDATORY FISH.
IT'S FIFTEEN FEET LONG, WITH A MENACING SET OF FANGS AND A VORACIOUS APPETITE TO MATCH.

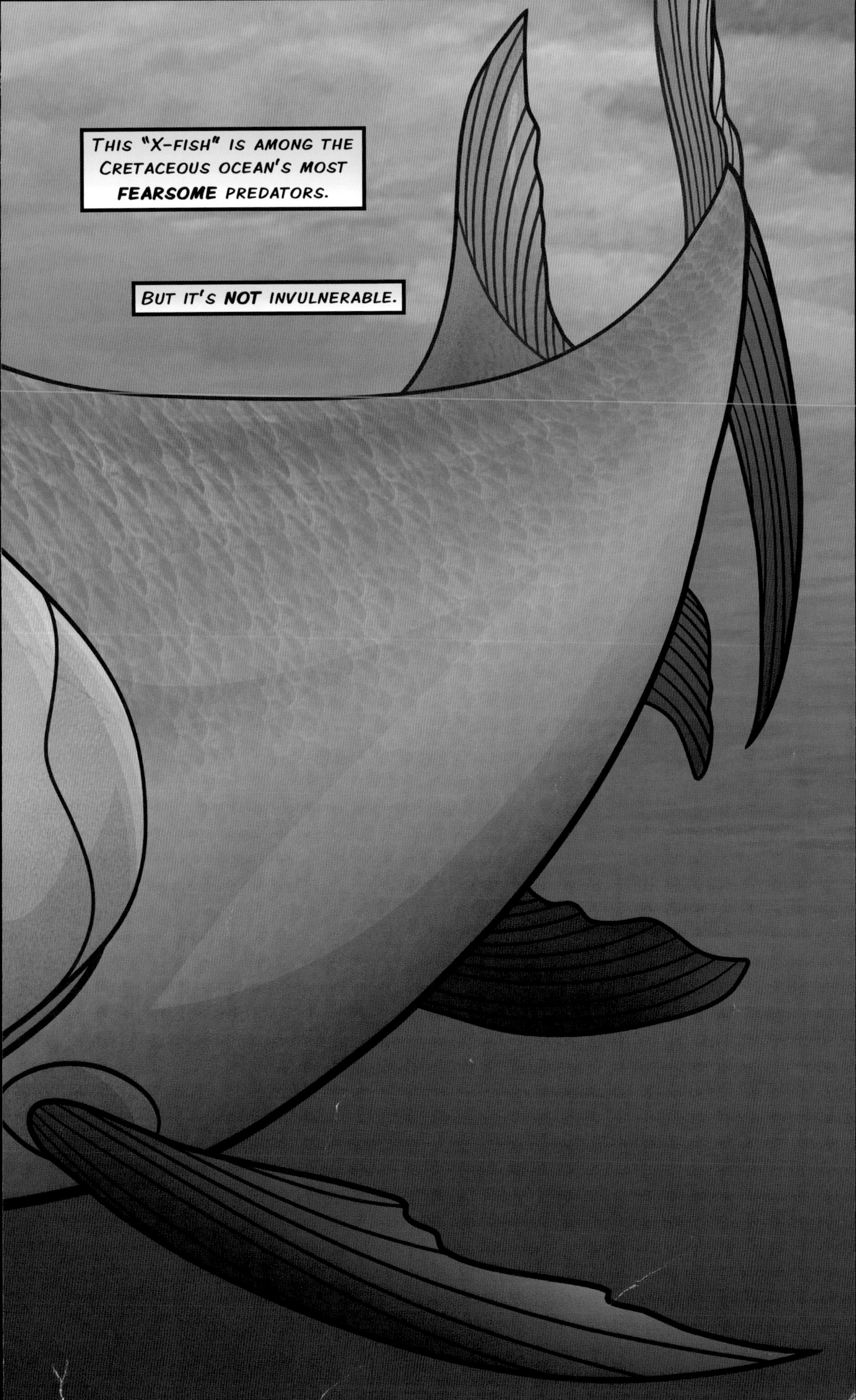
THIS "X-FISH" IS AMONG THE CRETACEOUS OCEAN'S MOST FEARSOME PREDATORS.
BUT IT'S NOT INVULNERABLE.

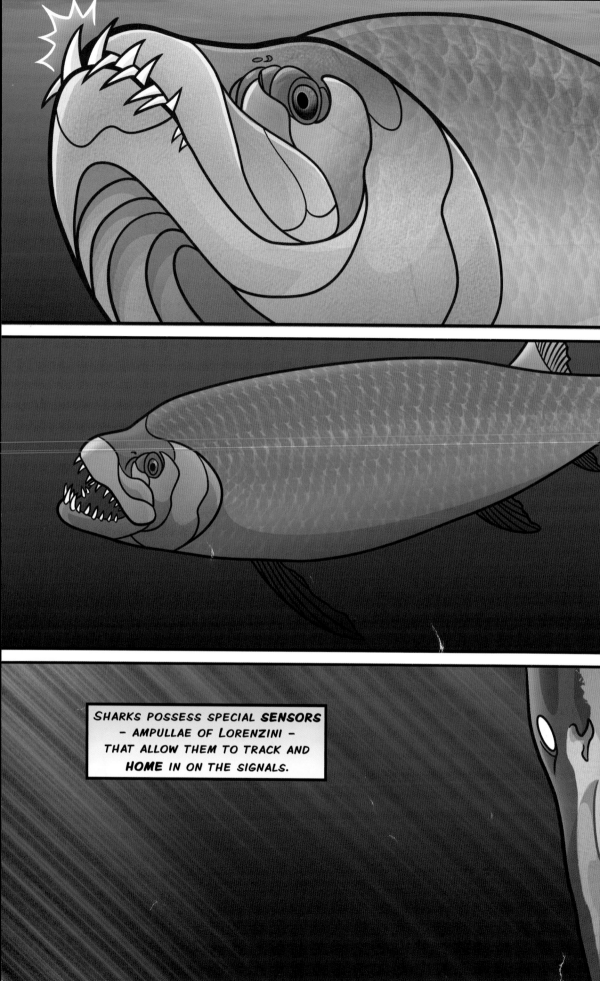

SHARKS POSSESS SPECIAL **SENSORS**
- AMPULLAE OF LORENZINI -
THAT ALLOW THEM TO TRACK AND
HOME IN ON THE SIGNALS.

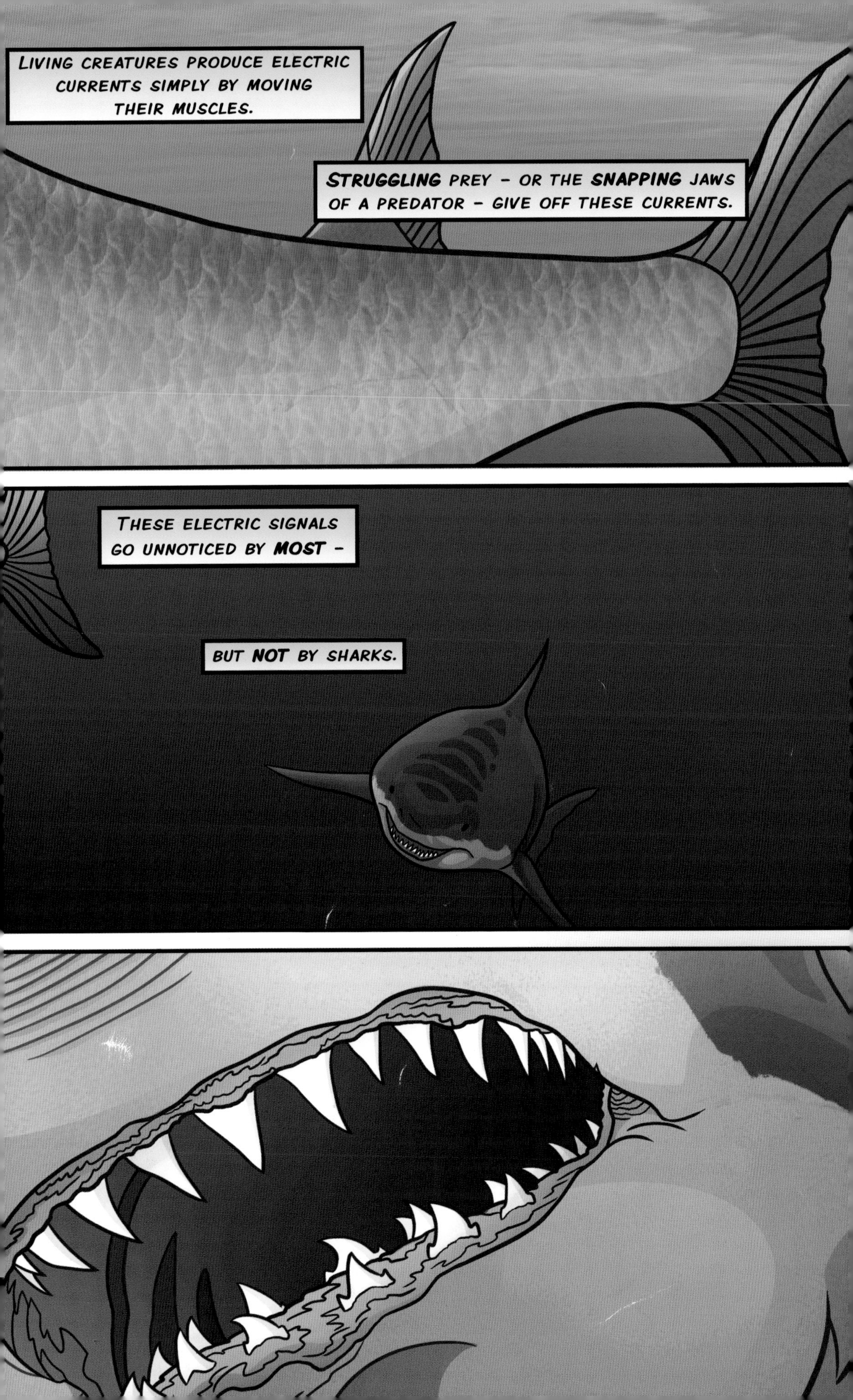
LIVING CREATURES PRODUCE ELECTRIC CURRENTS SIMPLY BY MOVING THEIR MUSCLES.
STRUGGLING PREY - OR THE SNAPPING JAWS OF A PREDATOR - GIVE OFF THESE CURRENTS.
THESE ELECTRIC SIGNALS GO UNNOTICED BY MOST -
BUT NOT BY SHARKS.

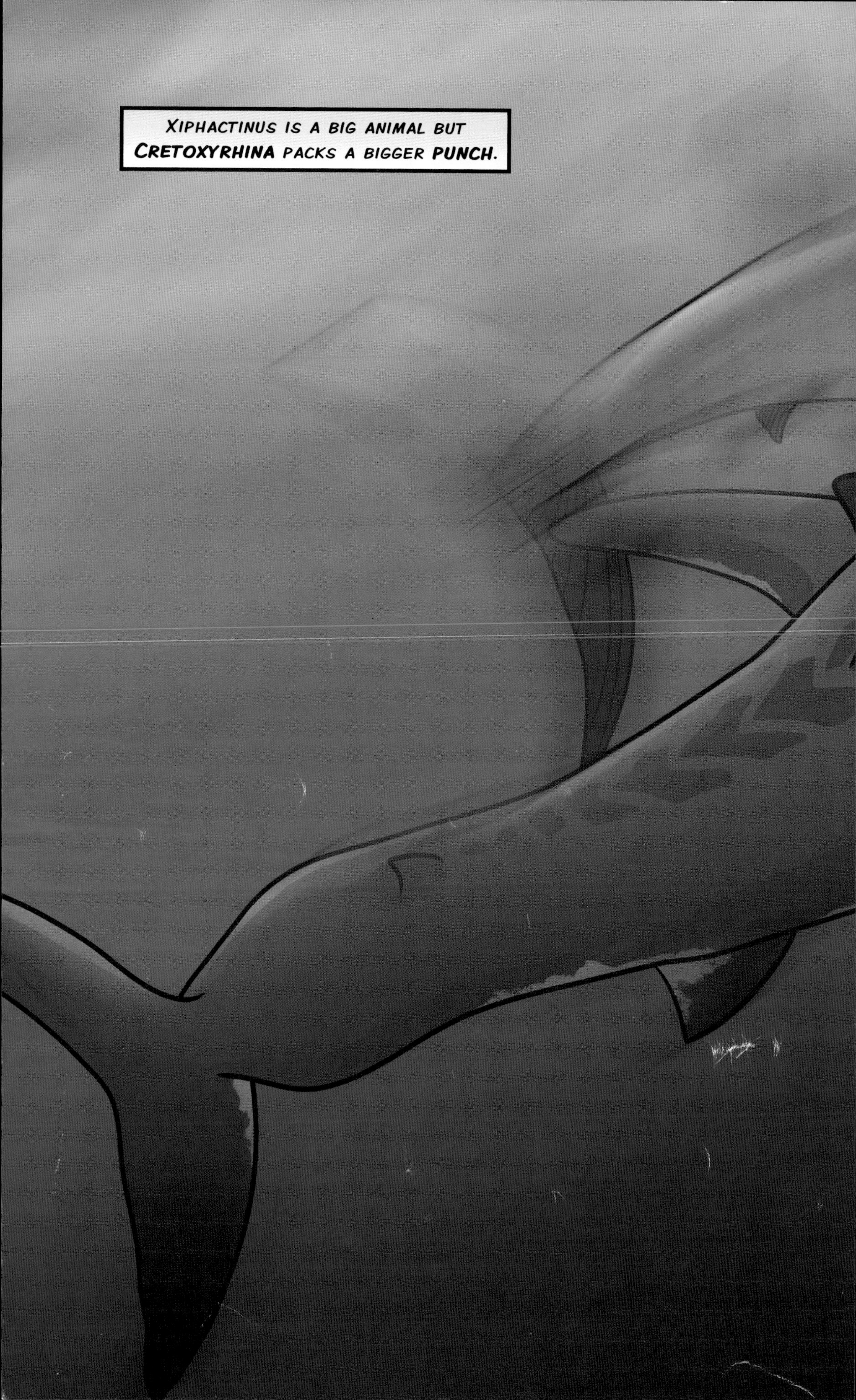
XIPHACTINUS IS A BIG ANIMAL BUT CRETOXYRHINA PACKS A BIGGER PUNCH.

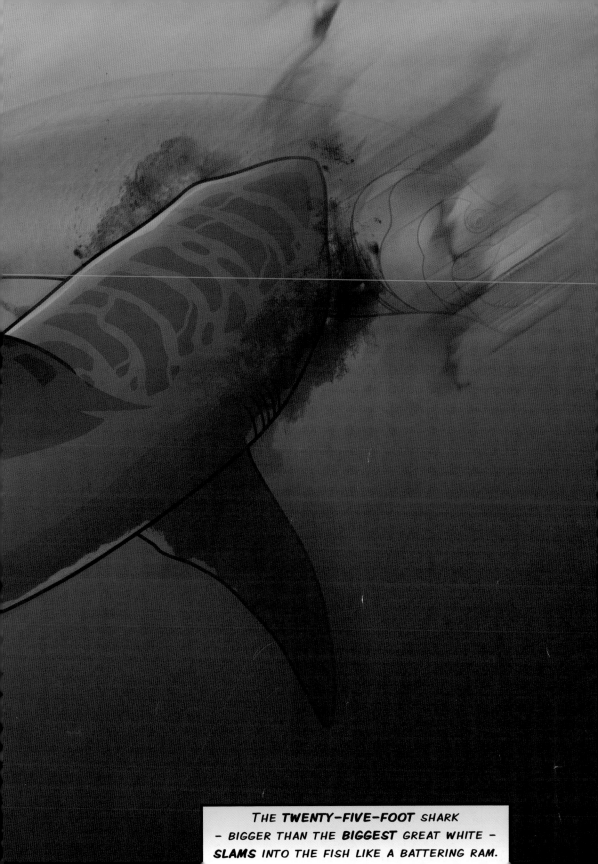

THE **TWENTY-FIVE-FOOT** SHARK
- BIGGER THAN THE **BIGGEST** GREAT WHITE -
SLAMS INTO THE FISH LIKE A BATTERING RAM.

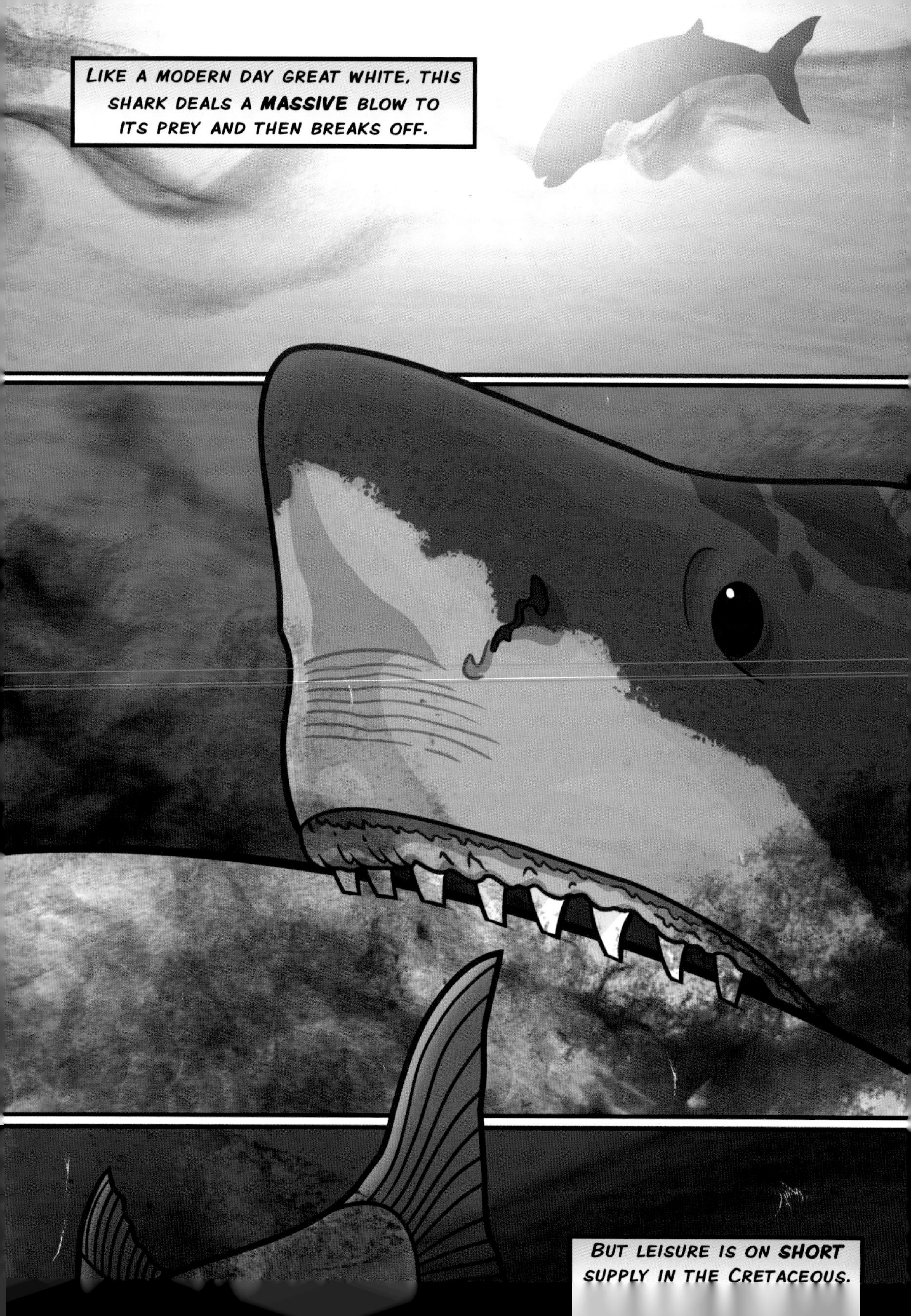
LIKE A MODERN DAY GREAT WHITE, THIS SHARK DEALS A **MASSIVE** BLOW TO ITS PREY AND THEN BREAKS OFF.
BUT LEISURE IS ON **SHORT** SUPPLY IN THE CRETACEOUS.

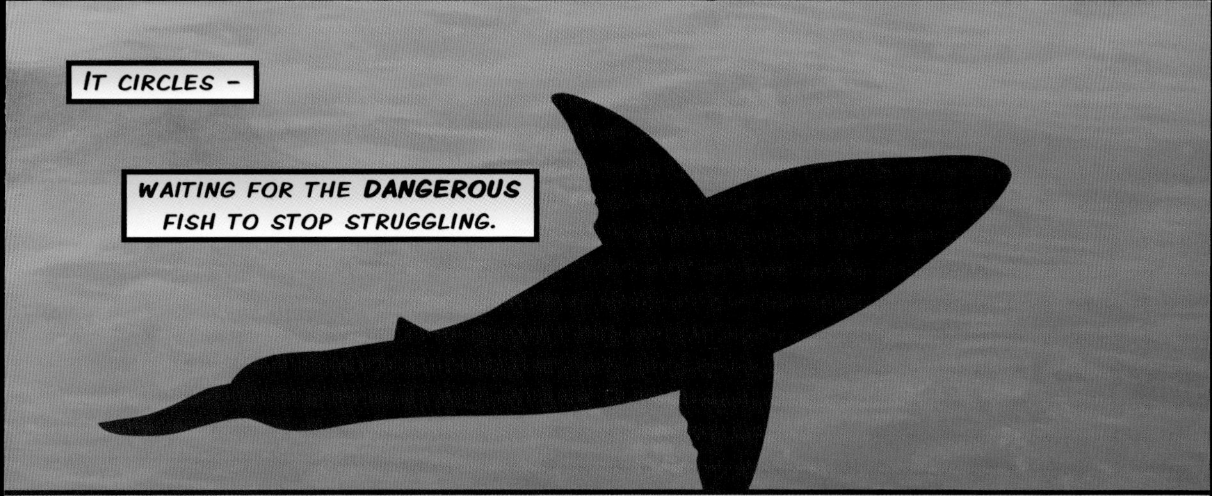
IT CIRCLES -
WAITING FOR THE DANGEROUS FISH TO STOP STRUGGLING.

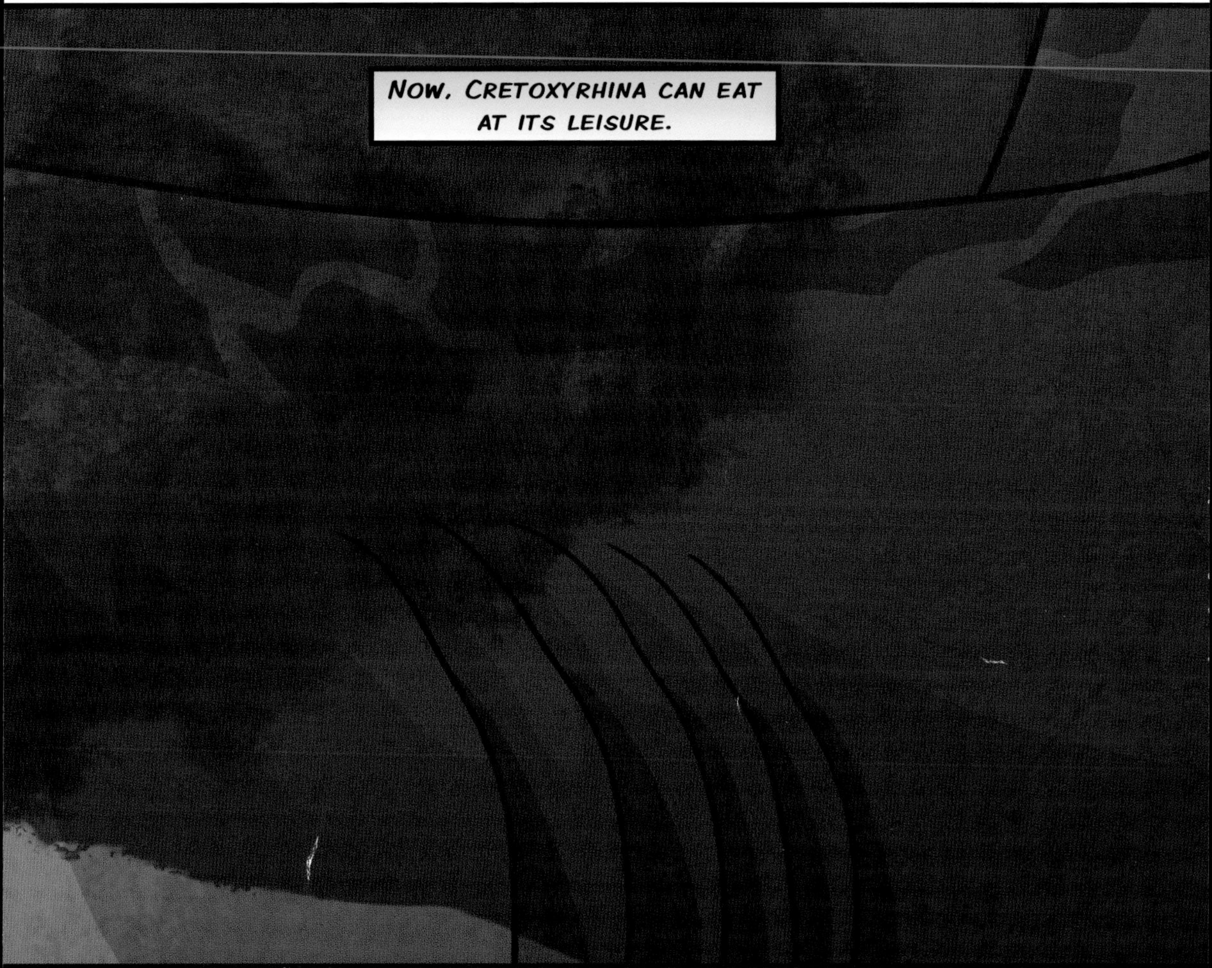
NOW, CRETOXYRHINA CAN EAT AT ITS LEISURE.

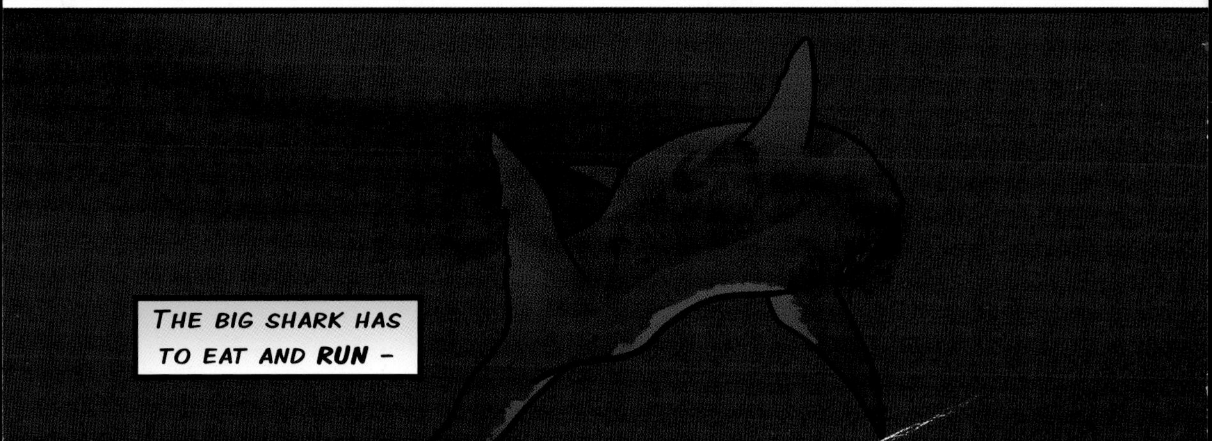
THE BIG SHARK HAS TO EAT AND RUN -

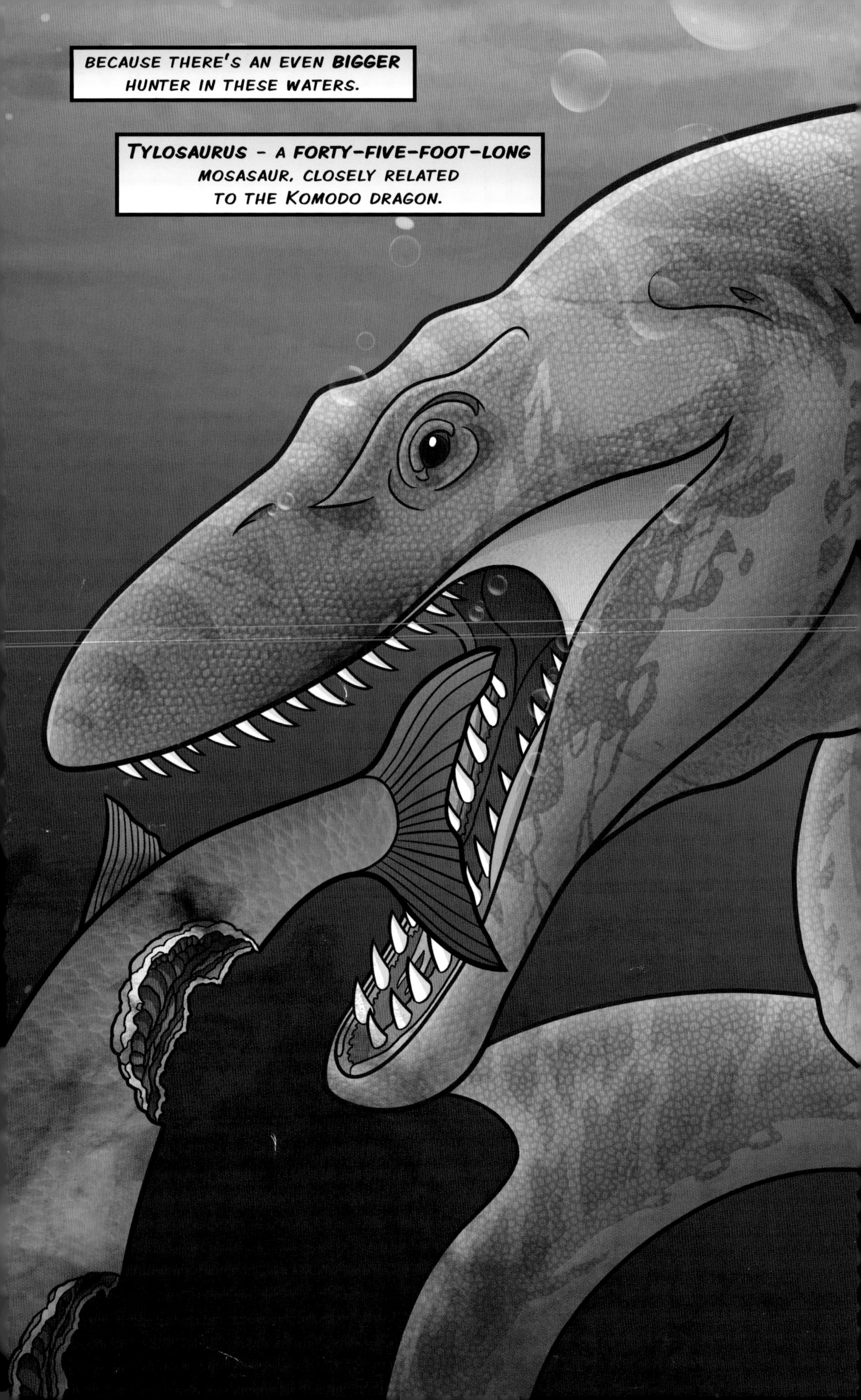
BECAUSE THERE'S AN EVEN BIGGER HUNTER IN THESE WATERS.
TYLOSAURUS - A FORTY-FIVE-FOOT-LONG MOSASAUR, CLOSELY RELATED TO THE KOMODO DRAGON.

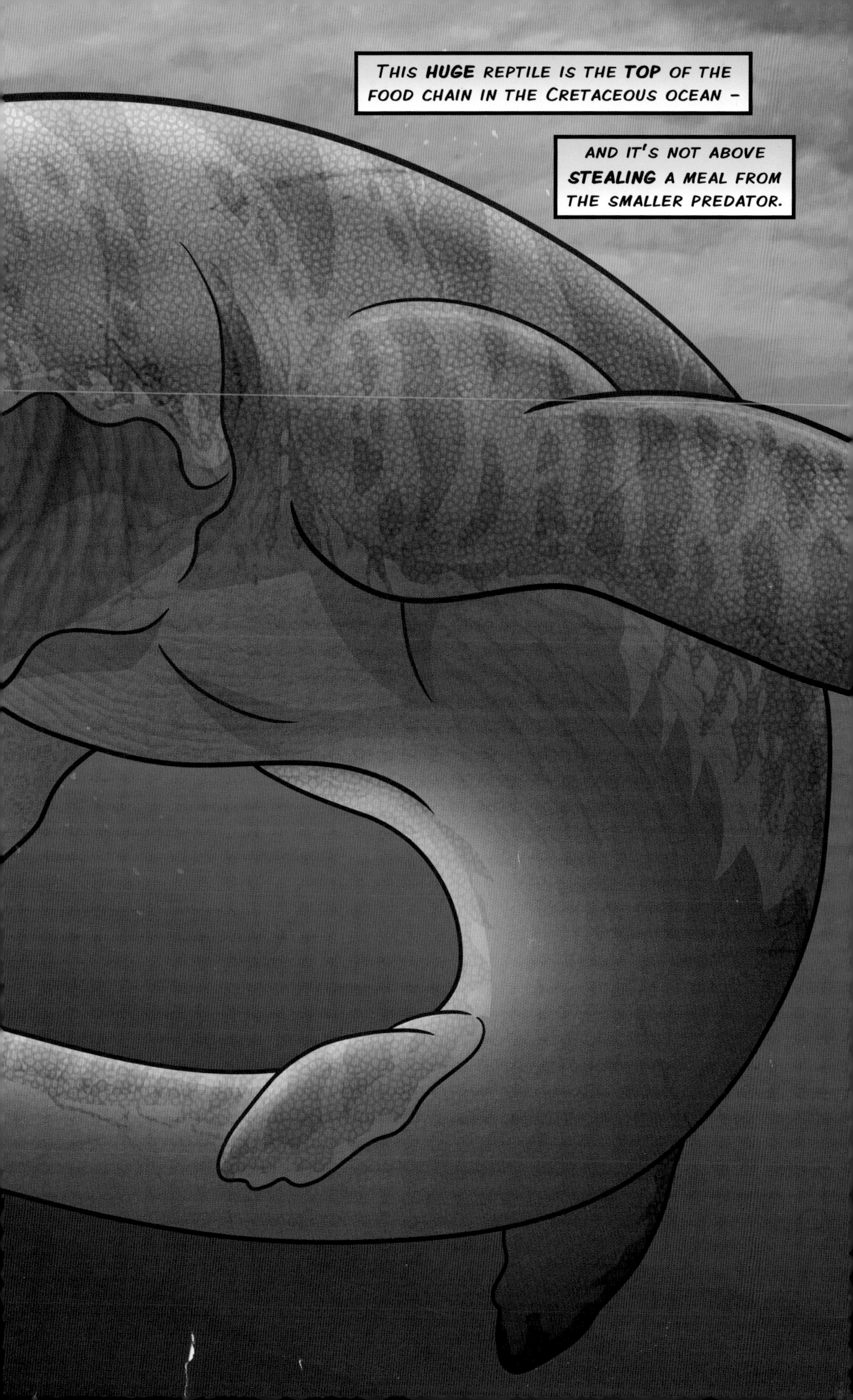
THIS HUGE REPTILE IS THE TOP OF THE FOOD CHAIN IN THE CRETACEOUS OCEAN –
AND IT'S NOT ABOVE STEALING A MEAL FROM THE SMALLER PREDATOR.

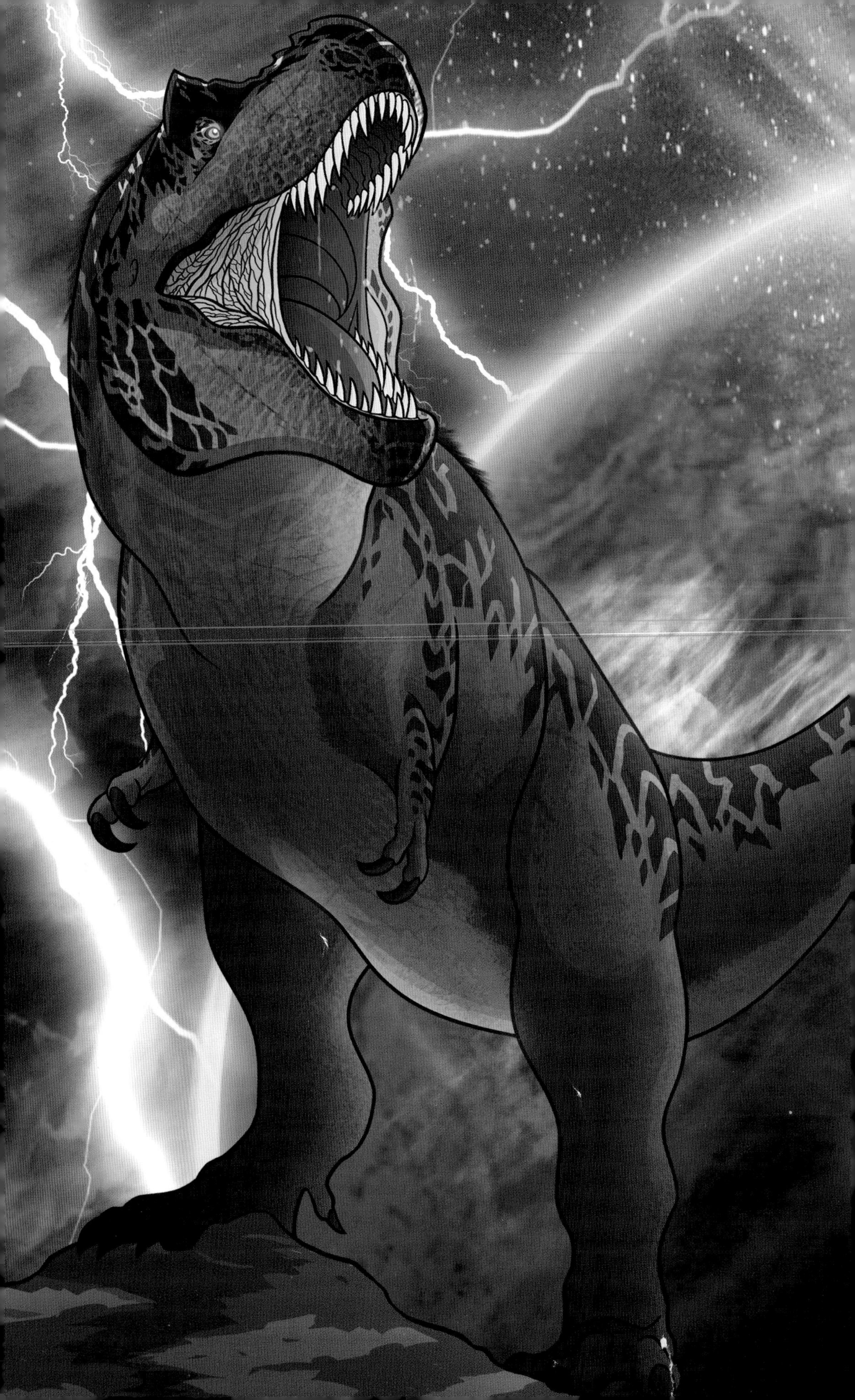

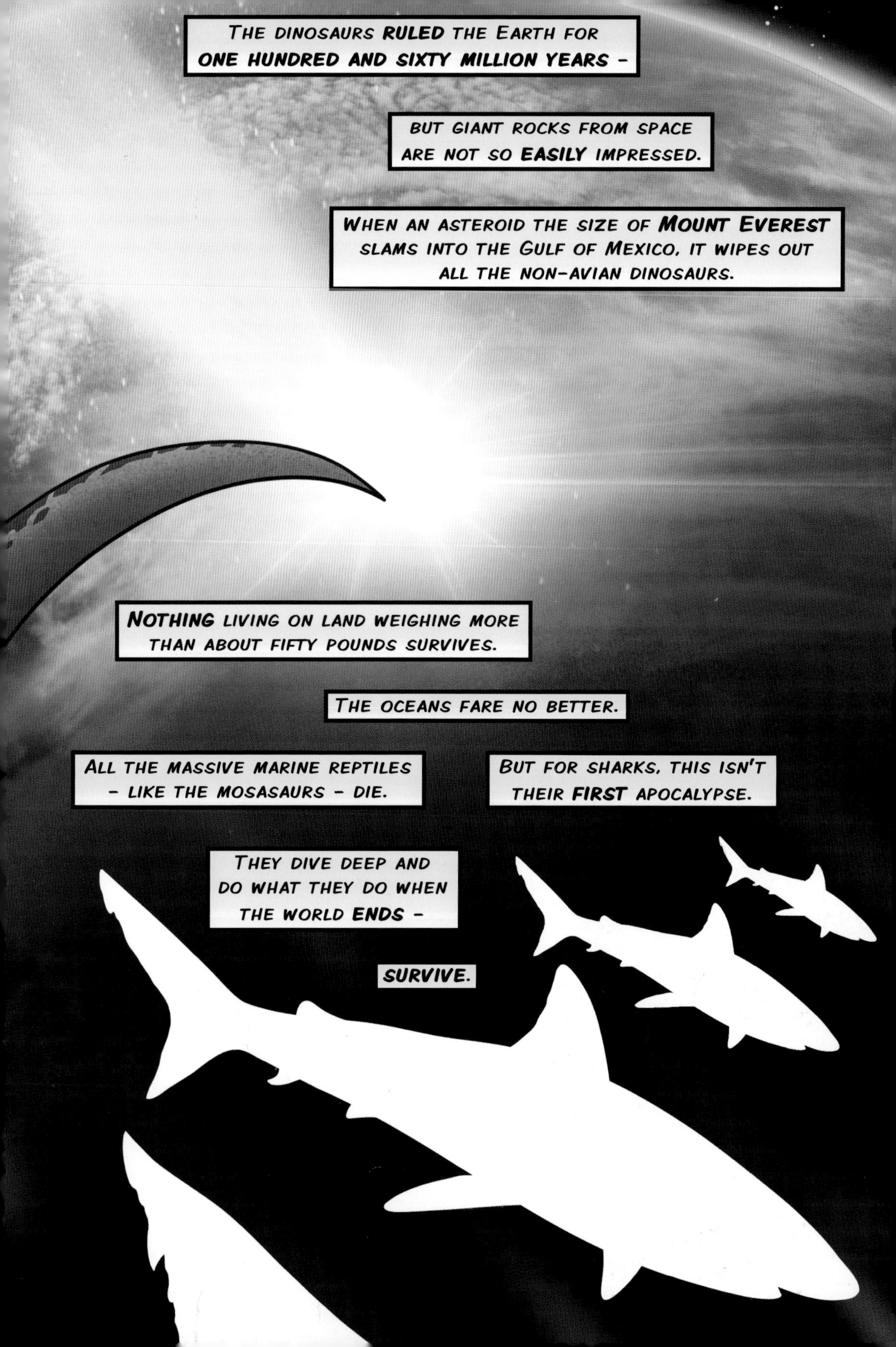
THE DINOSAURS RULED THE EARTH FOR ONE HUNDRED AND SIXTY MILLION YEARS -
BUT GIANT ROCKS FROM SPACE ARE NOT SO EASILY IMPRESSED.
WHEN AN ASTEROID THE SIZE OF MOUNT EVEREST SLAMS INTO THE GULF OF MEXICO, IT WIPES OUT ALL THE NON-AVIAN DINOSAURS.
NOTHING LIVING ON LAND WEIGHING MORE THAN ABOUT FIFTY POUNDS SURVIVES.
THE OCEANS FARE NO BETTER.
ALL THE MASSIVE MARINE REPTILES - LIKE THE MOSASAURS - DIE.
BUT FOR SHARKS, THIS ISN'T THEIR FIRST APOCALYPSE.
THEY DIVE DEEP AND DO WHAT THEY DO WHEN THE WORLD ENDS -
SURVIVE.

PART THREE
CENOZOIC

66 - 0
MILLION YEARS AGO

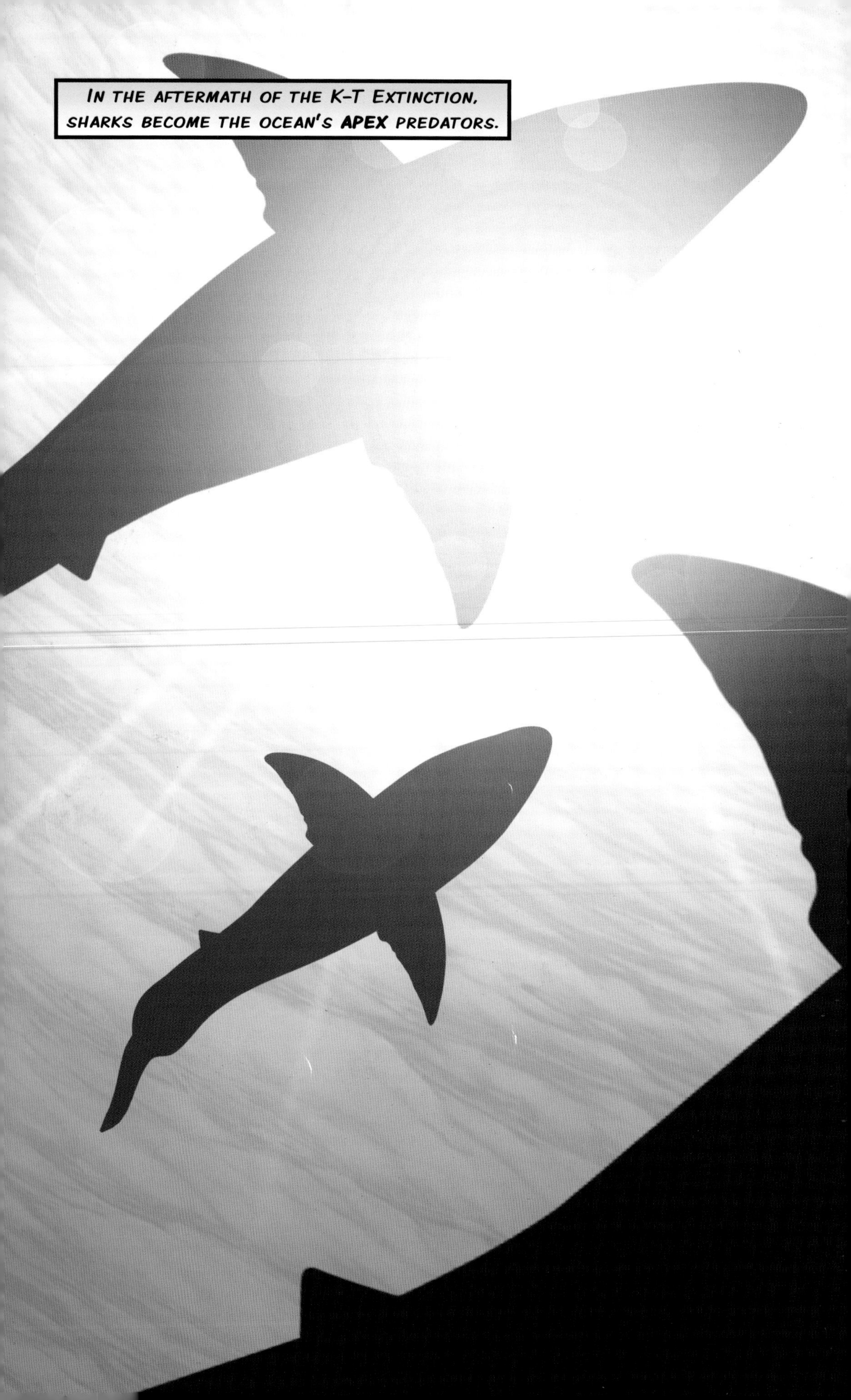
In the aftermath of the K-T Extinction, sharks become the ocean's **APEX** predators.

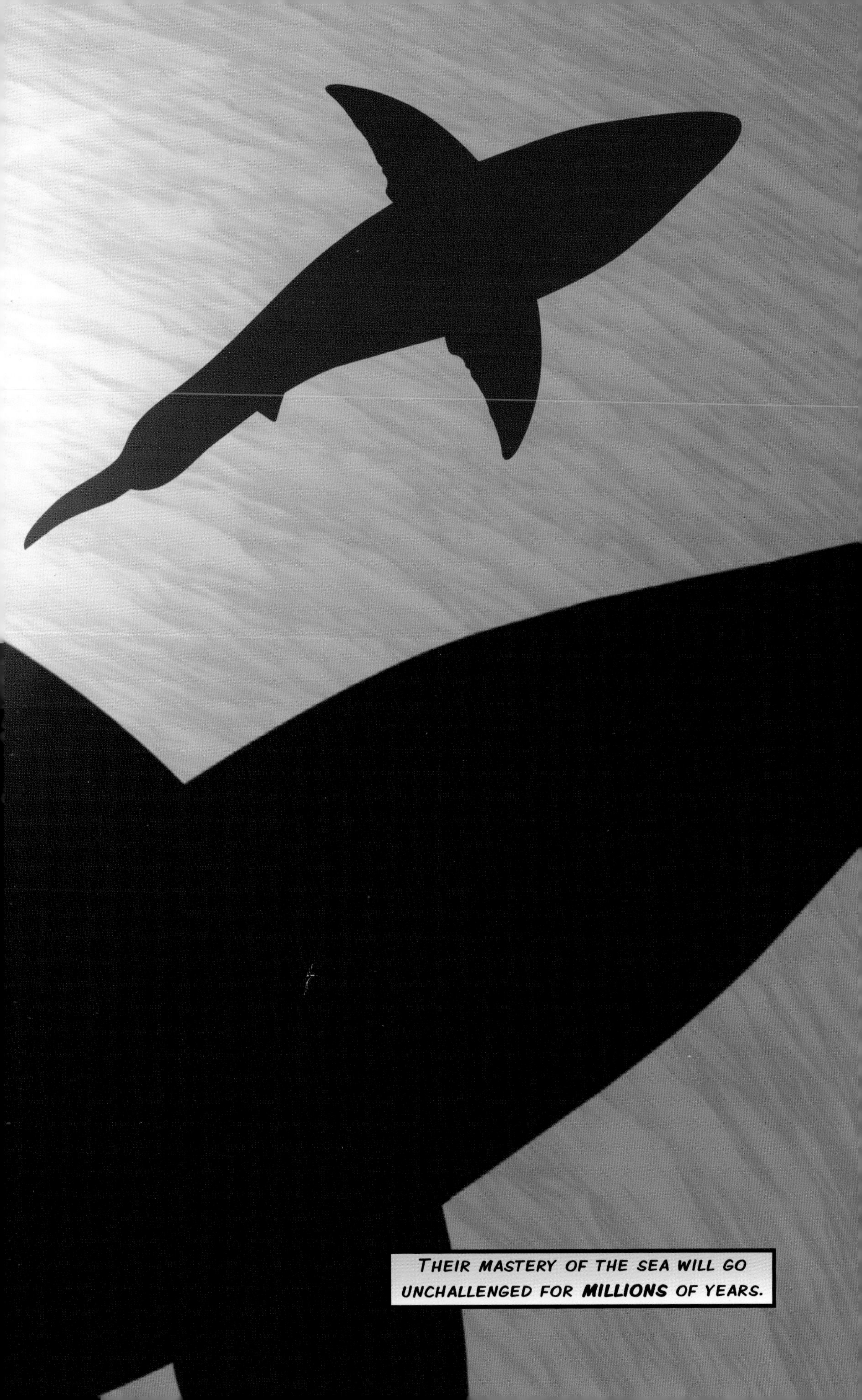
THEIR MASTERY OF THE SEA WILL GO UNCHALLENGED FOR **MILLIONS** OF YEARS.

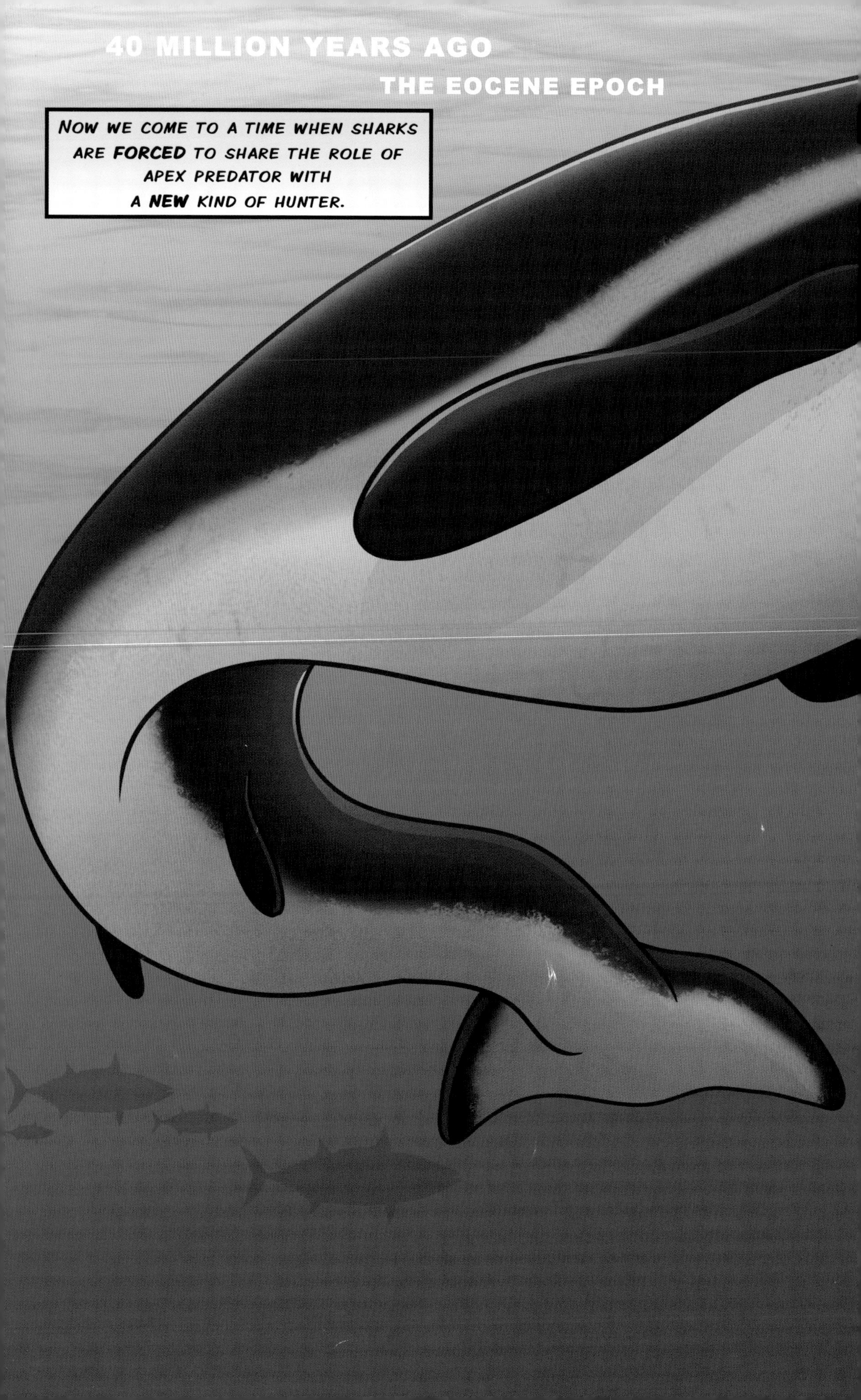

40 MILLION YEARS AGO
THE EOCENE EPOCH
NOW WE COME TO A TIME WHEN SHARKS ARE FORCED TO SHARE THE ROLE OF APEX PREDATOR WITH A NEW KIND OF HUNTER.

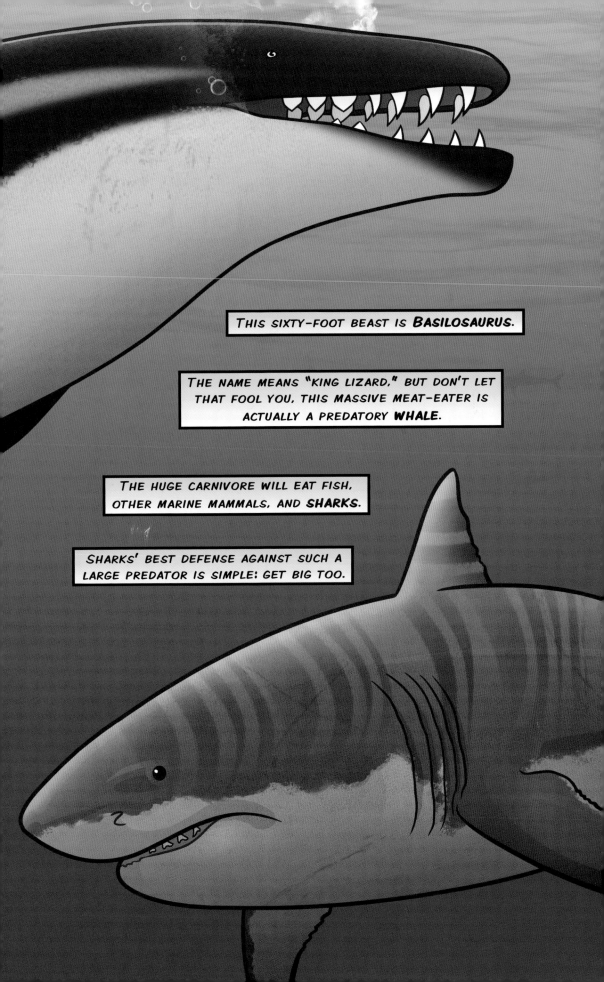

This sixty-foot beast is **Basilosaurus**.

The name means "king lizard," but don't let that fool you, this massive meat-eater is actually a predatory **whale**.

The huge carnivore will eat fish, other marine mammals, and **sharks**.

Sharks' best defense against such a large predator is simple: get big too.

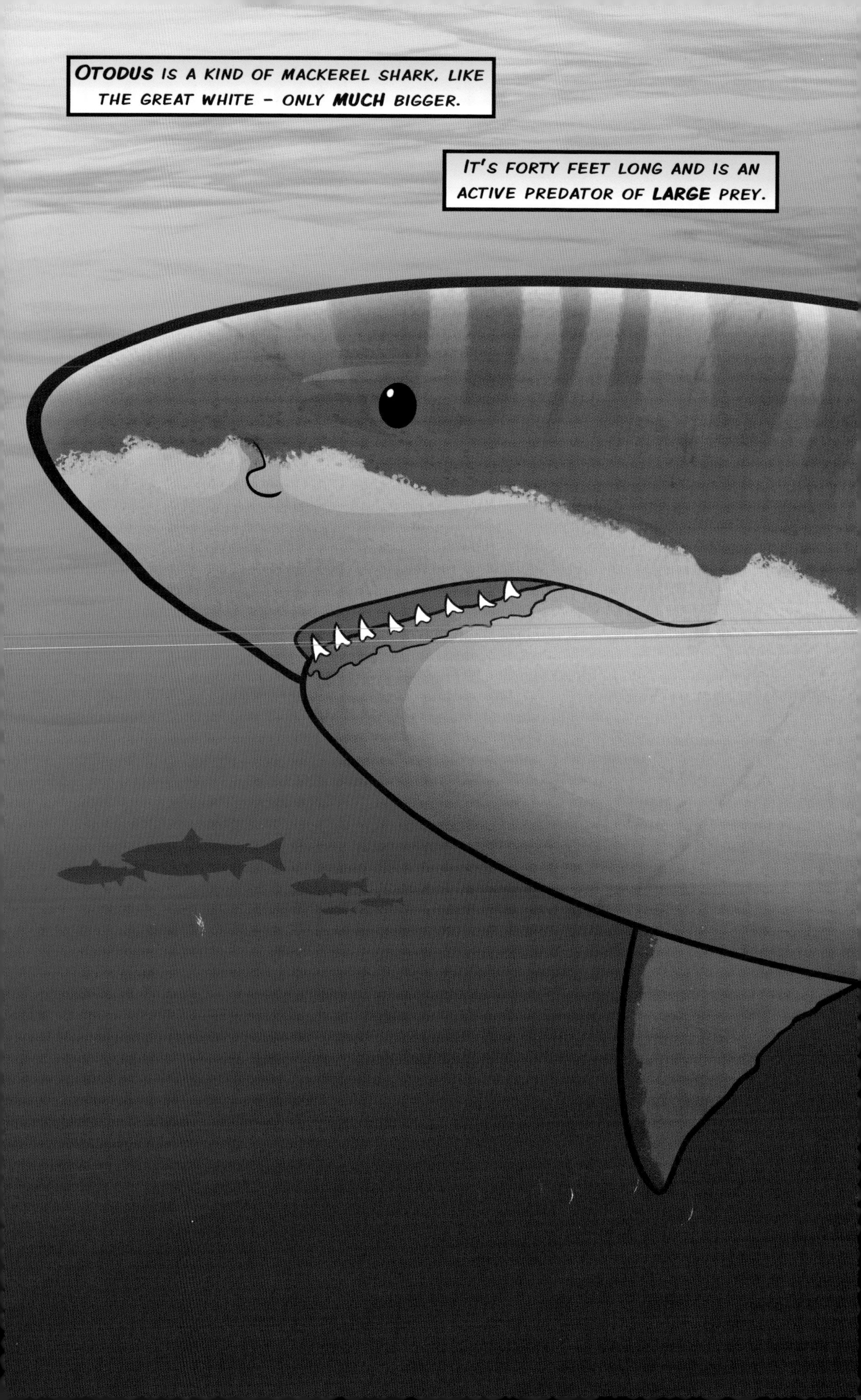
OTODUS IS A KIND OF MACKEREL SHARK, LIKE THE GREAT WHITE – ONLY MUCH BIGGER.
IT'S FORTY FEET LONG AND IS AN ACTIVE PREDATOR OF LARGE PREY.

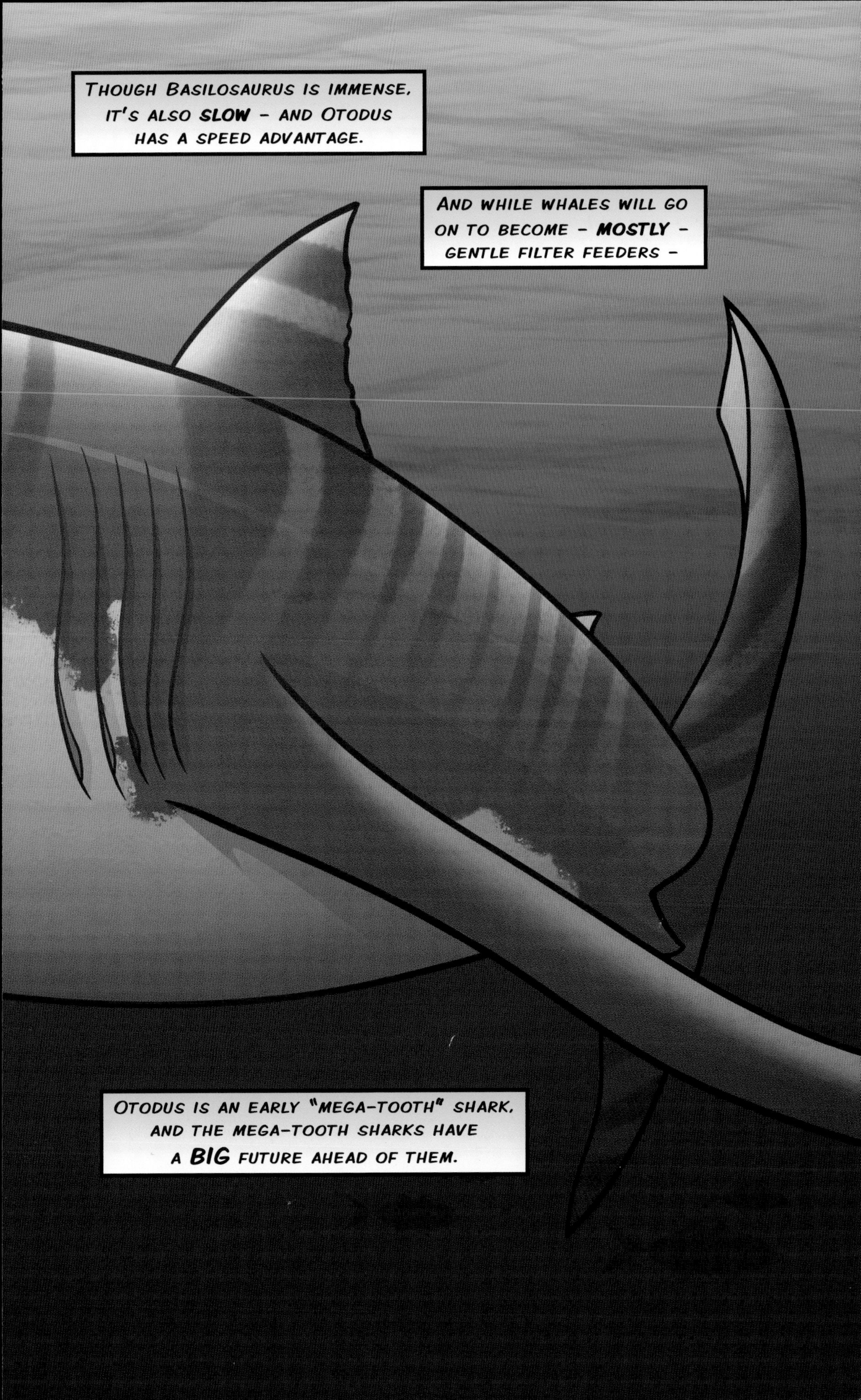

Though Basilosaurus is immense, it's also **SLOW** – and Otodus has a speed advantage.
And while whales will go on to become – **MOSTLY** – gentle filter feeders –
Otodus is an early "mega-tooth" shark, and the mega-tooth sharks have a **BIG** future ahead of them.

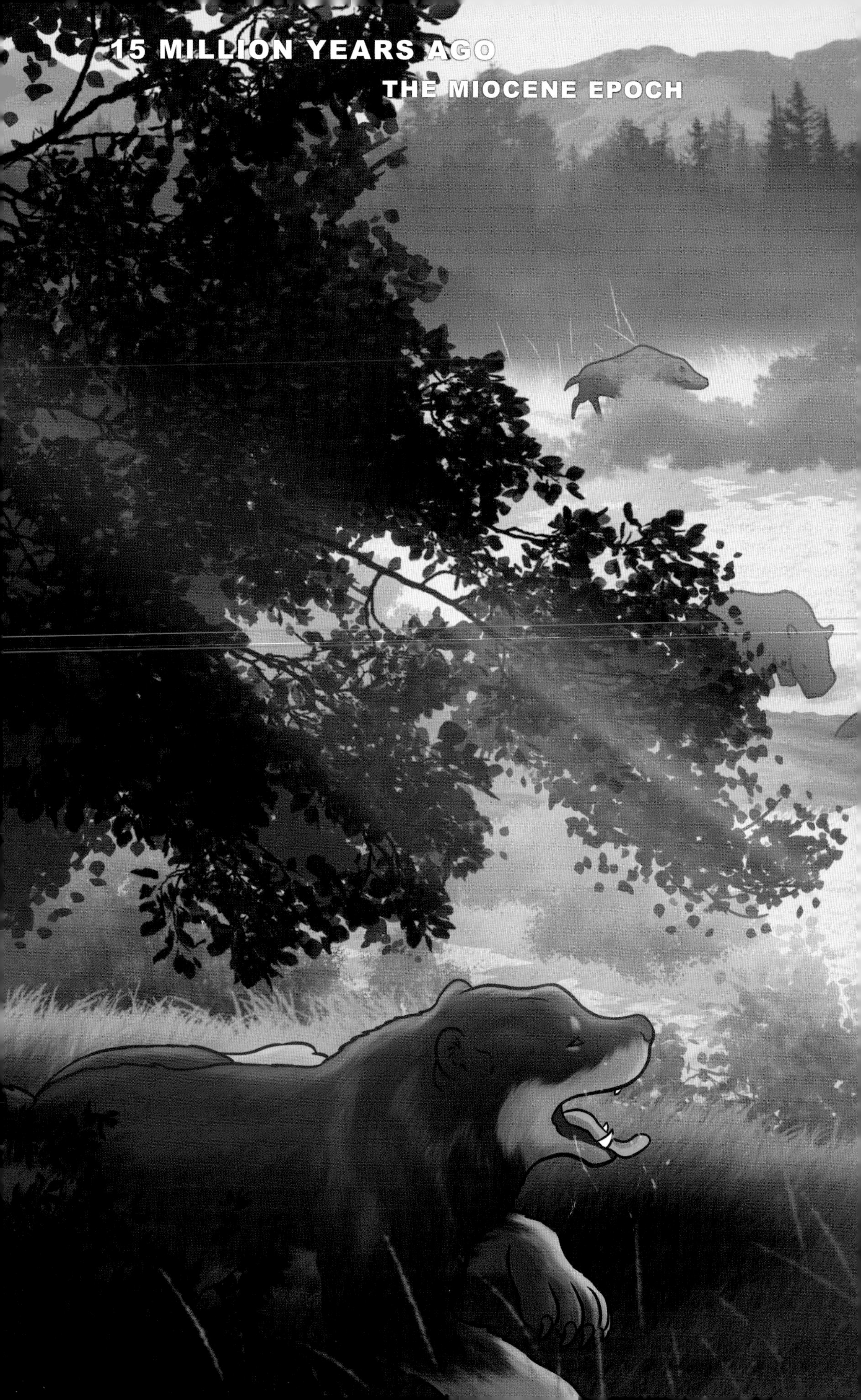
15 MILLION YEARS AGO
THE MIOCENE EPOCH

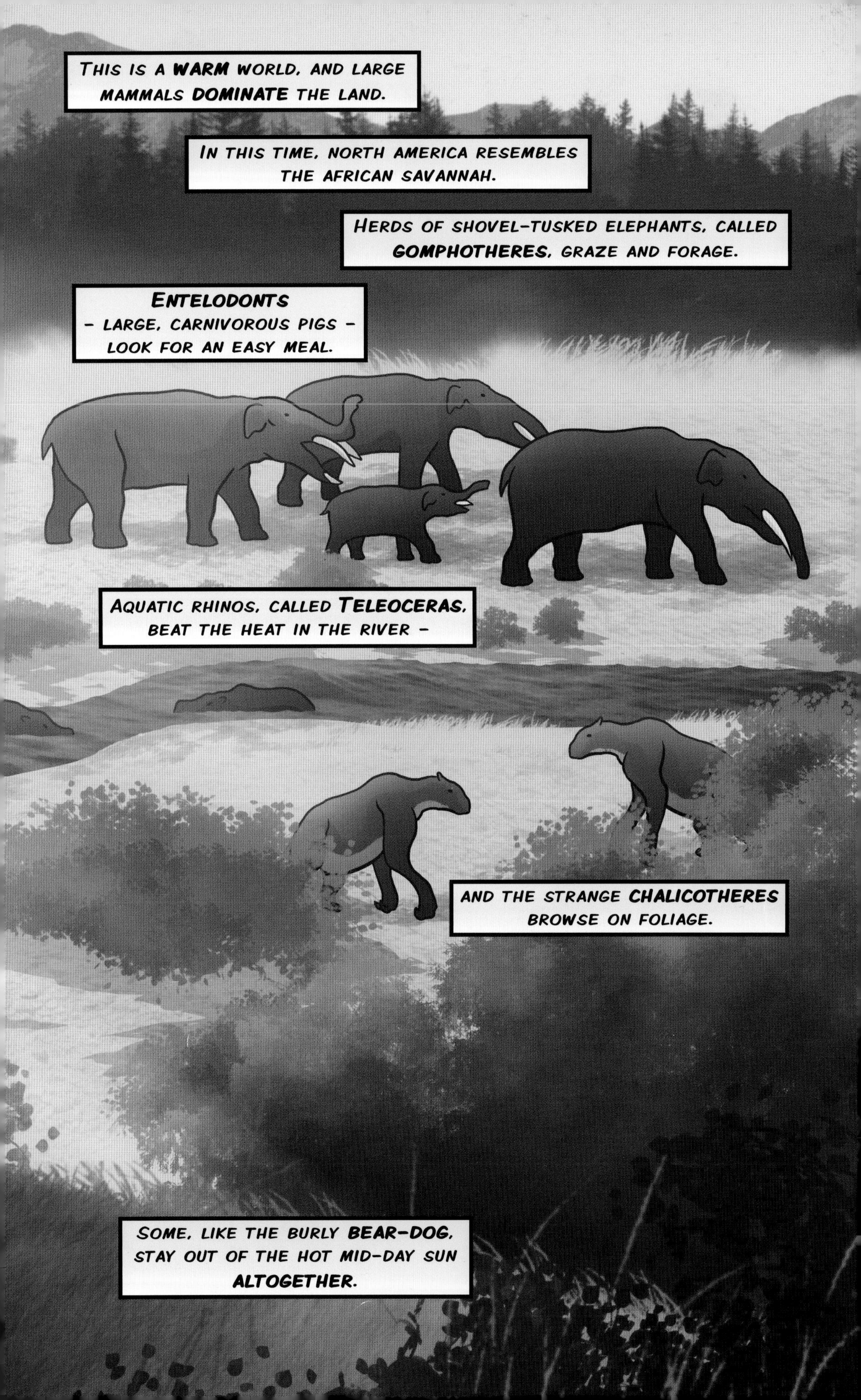
THIS IS A WARM WORLD, AND LARGE MAMMALS DOMINATE THE LAND.
IN THIS TIME, NORTH AMERICA RESEMBLES THE AFRICAN SAVANNAH.
HERDS OF SHOVEL-TUSKED ELEPHANTS, CALLED GOMPHOTHERES, GRAZE AND FORAGE.
ENTELODONTS - LARGE, CARNIVOROUS PIGS - LOOK FOR AN EASY MEAL.
AQUATIC RHINOS, CALLED TELEOCERAS, BEAT THE HEAT IN THE RIVER -
AND THE STRANGE CHALICOTHERES BROWSE ON FOLIAGE.
SOME, LIKE THE BURLY BEAR-DOG, STAY OUT OF THE HOT MID-DAY SUN ALTOGETHER.

MAMMALS RULE THE LAND, WITHOUT QUESTION –

THESE BALEEN WHALES ARE OVER THIRTY FEET LONG – SOME OVER **FORTY**.

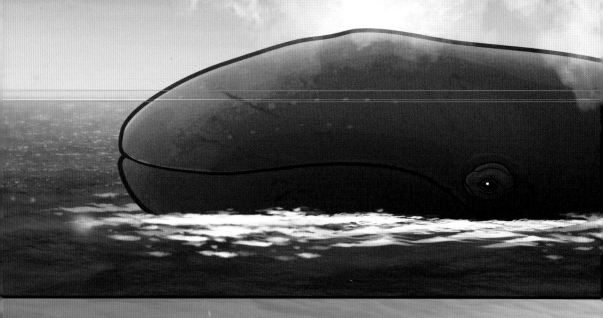

IN THE MIOCENE OCEAN, THERE'S **NO** SUCH THING AS "BIG ENOUGH" TO BE SAFE.

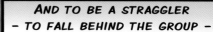

AND TO BE A STRAGGLER – TO FALL BEHIND THE GROUP –

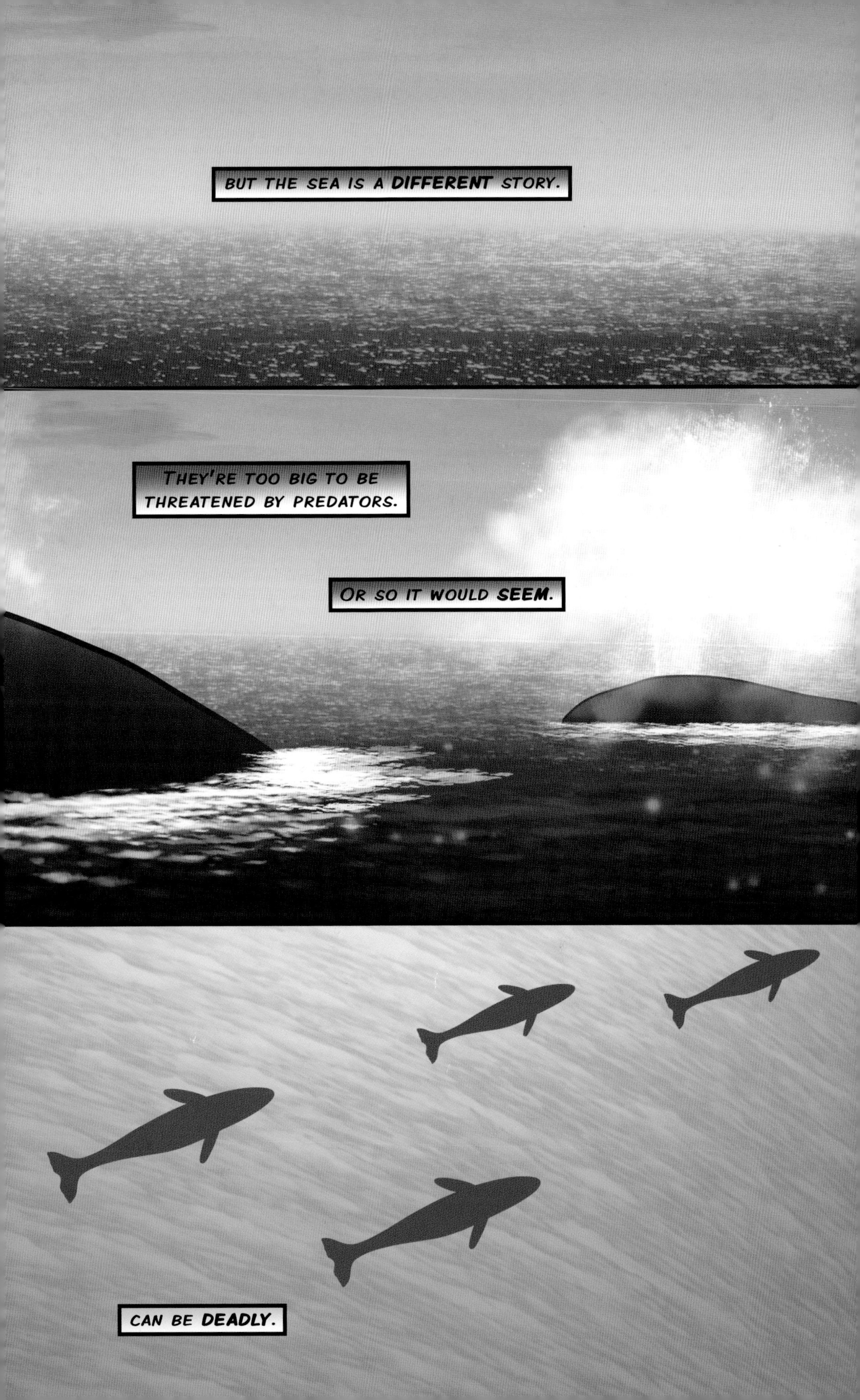
BUT THE SEA IS A DIFFERENT STORY.
THEY'RE TOO BIG TO BE THREATENED BY PREDATORS.
OR SO IT WOULD SEEM.
CAN BE DEADLY.

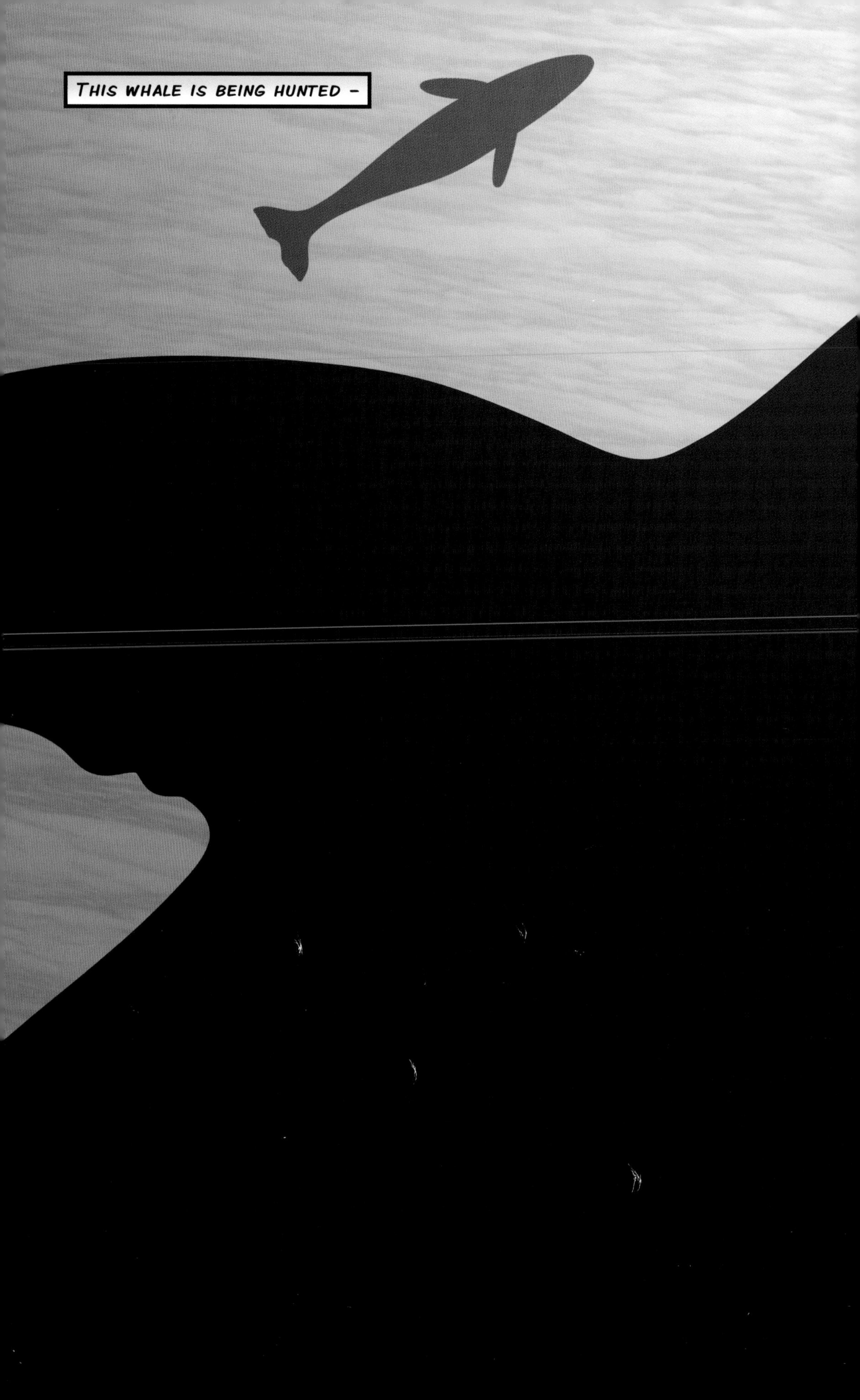
THIS WHALE IS BEING HUNTED -

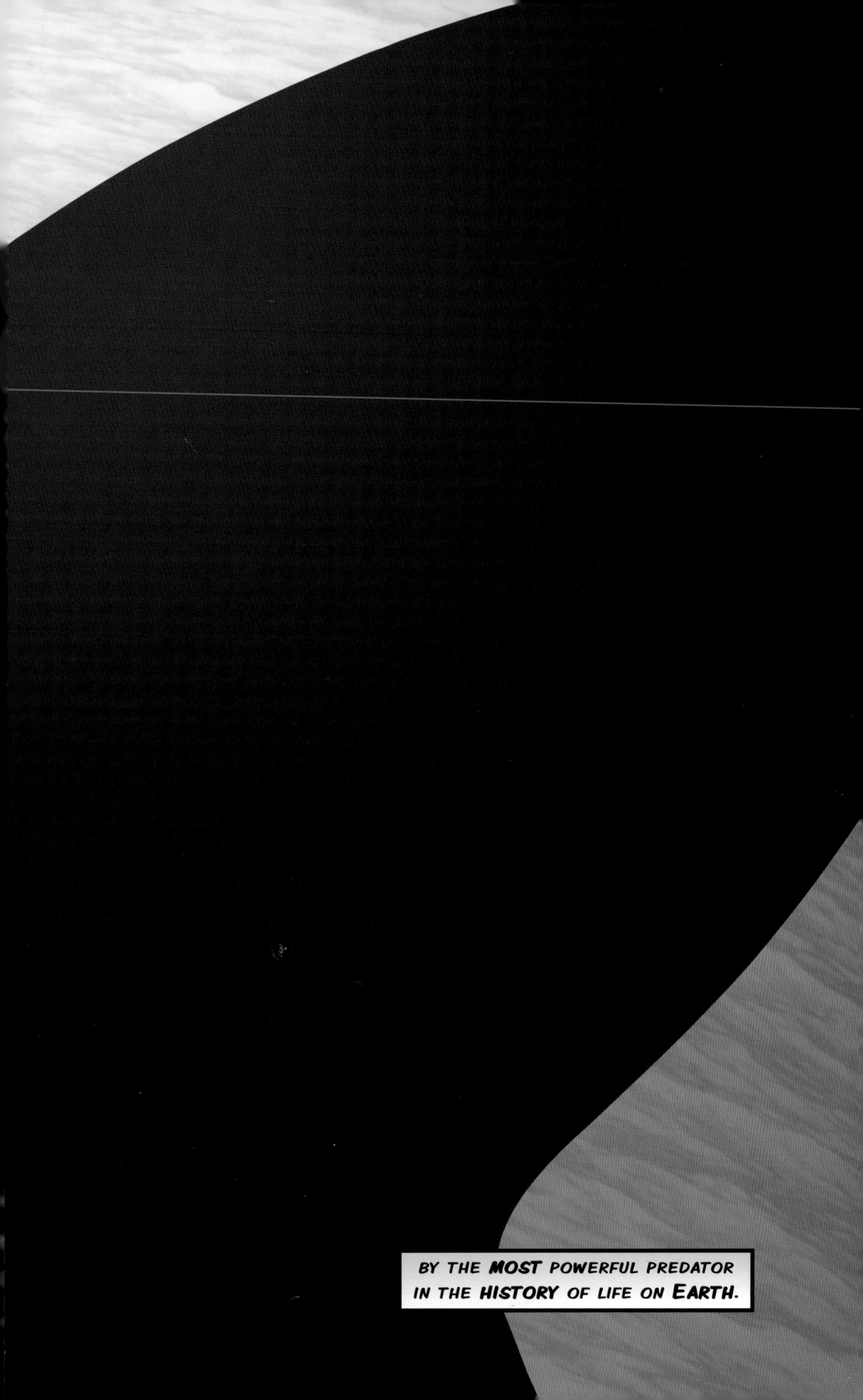
BY THE MOST POWERFUL PREDATOR IN THE HISTORY OF LIFE ON EARTH.

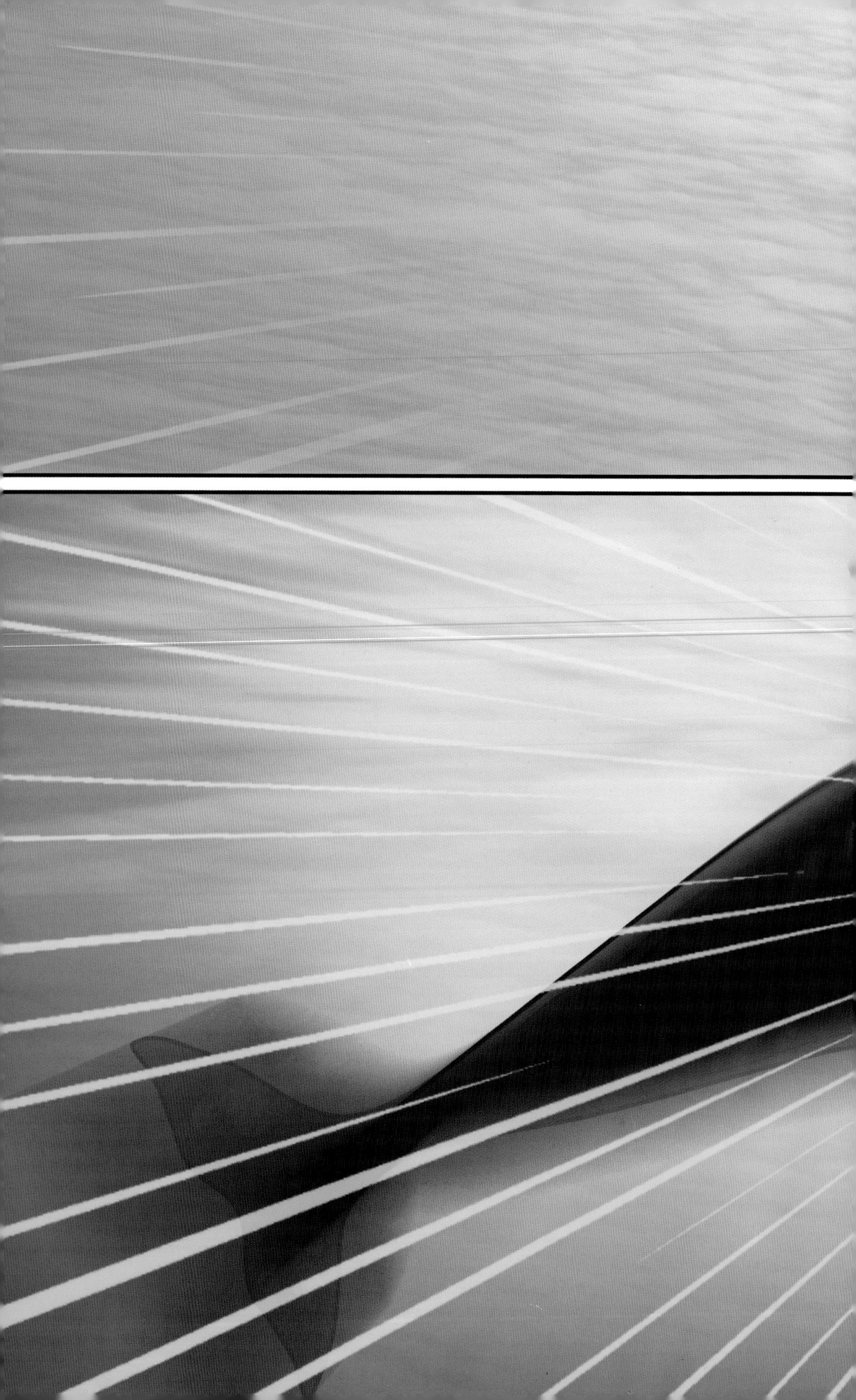

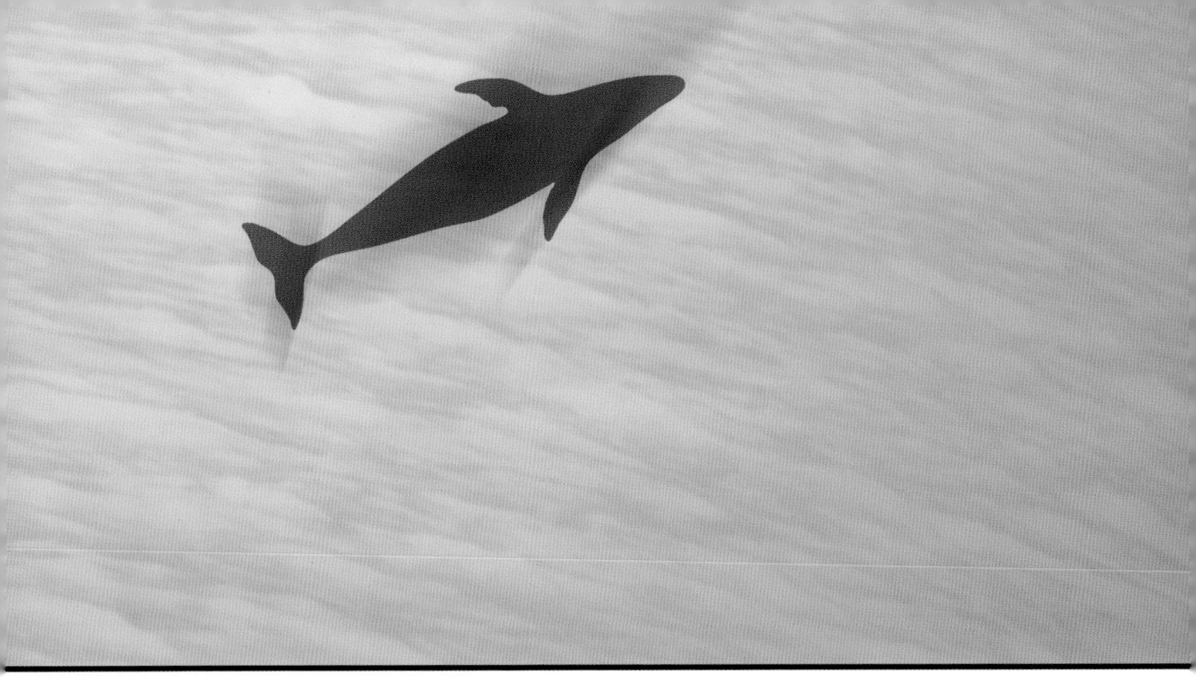

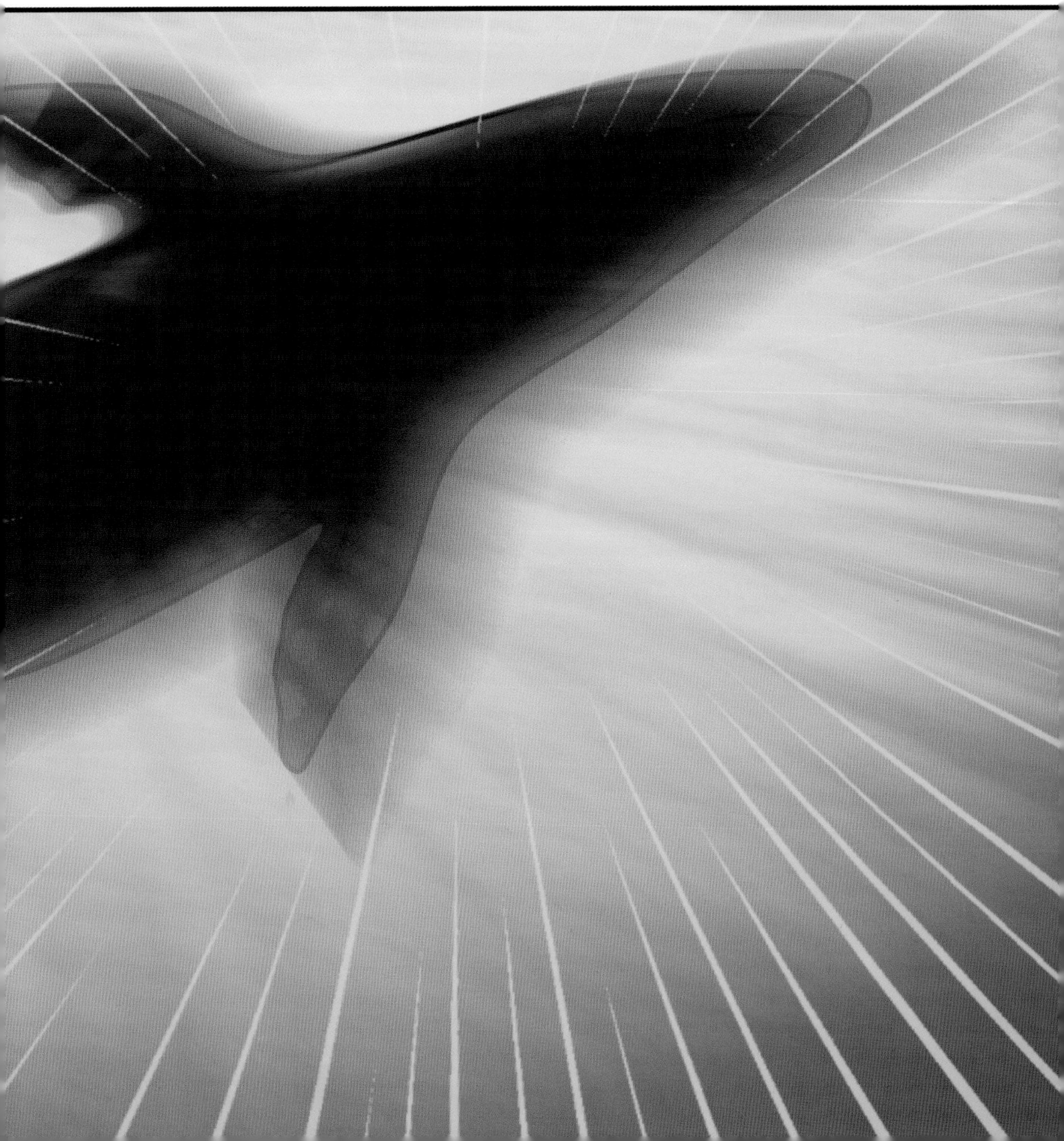

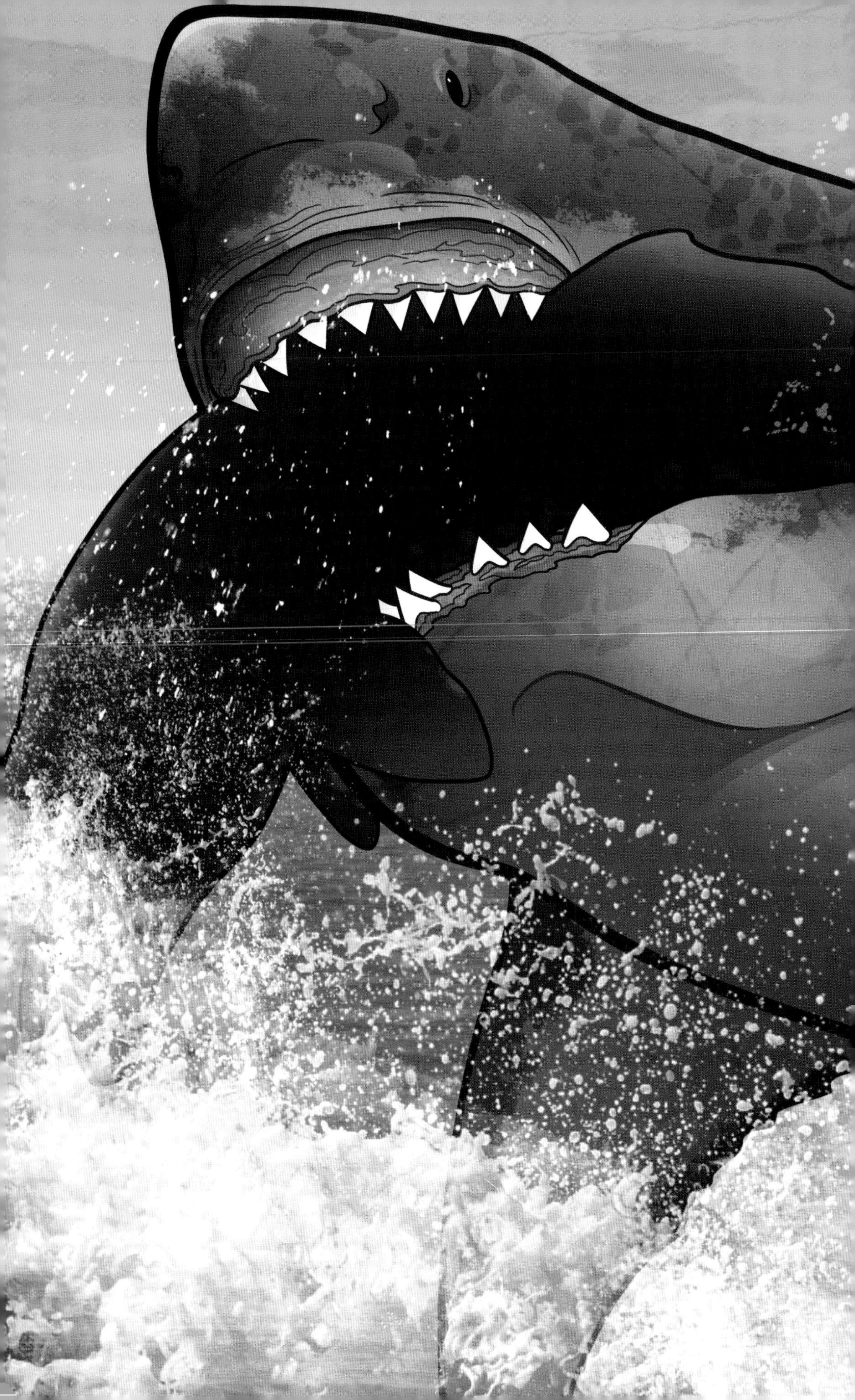

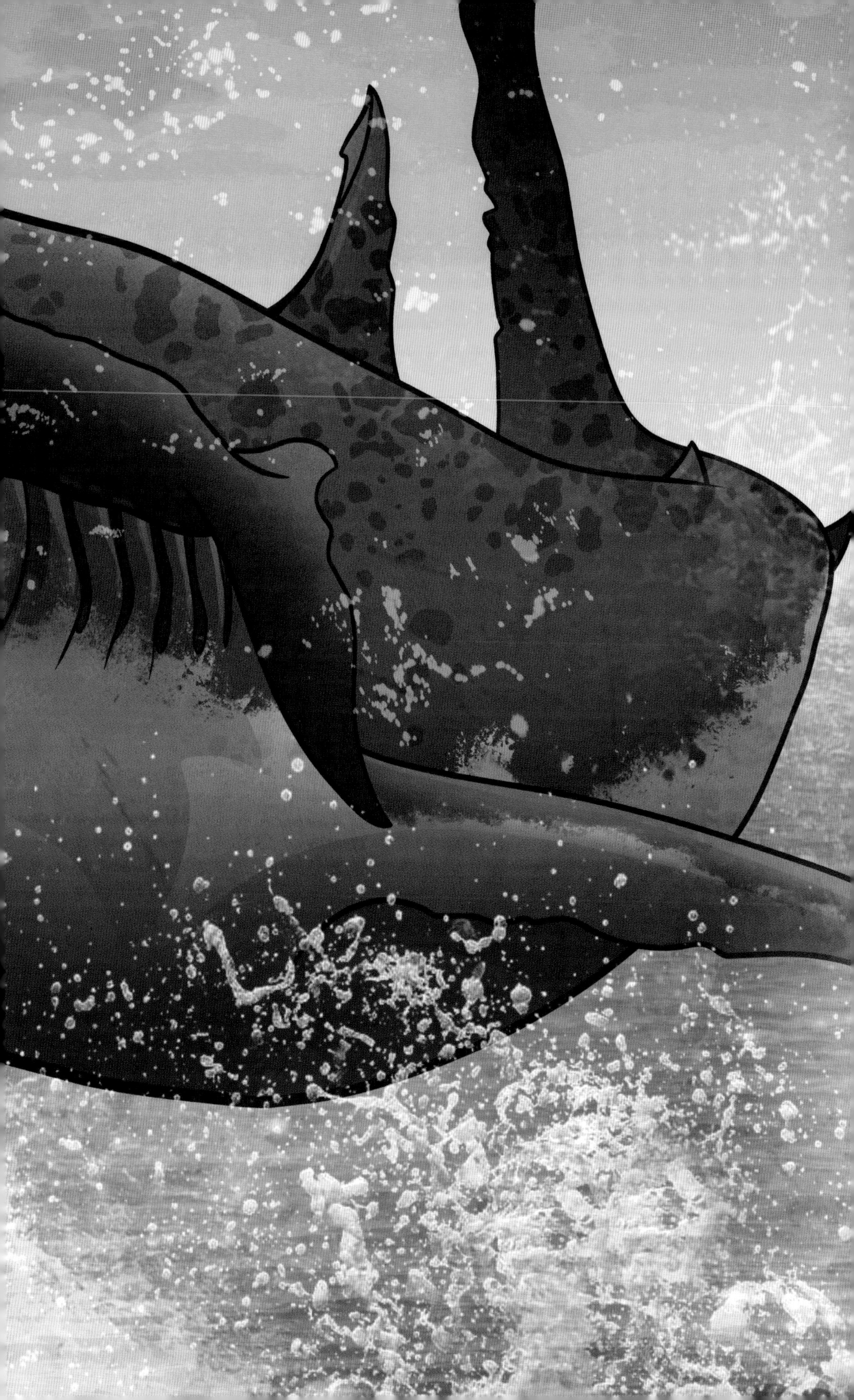

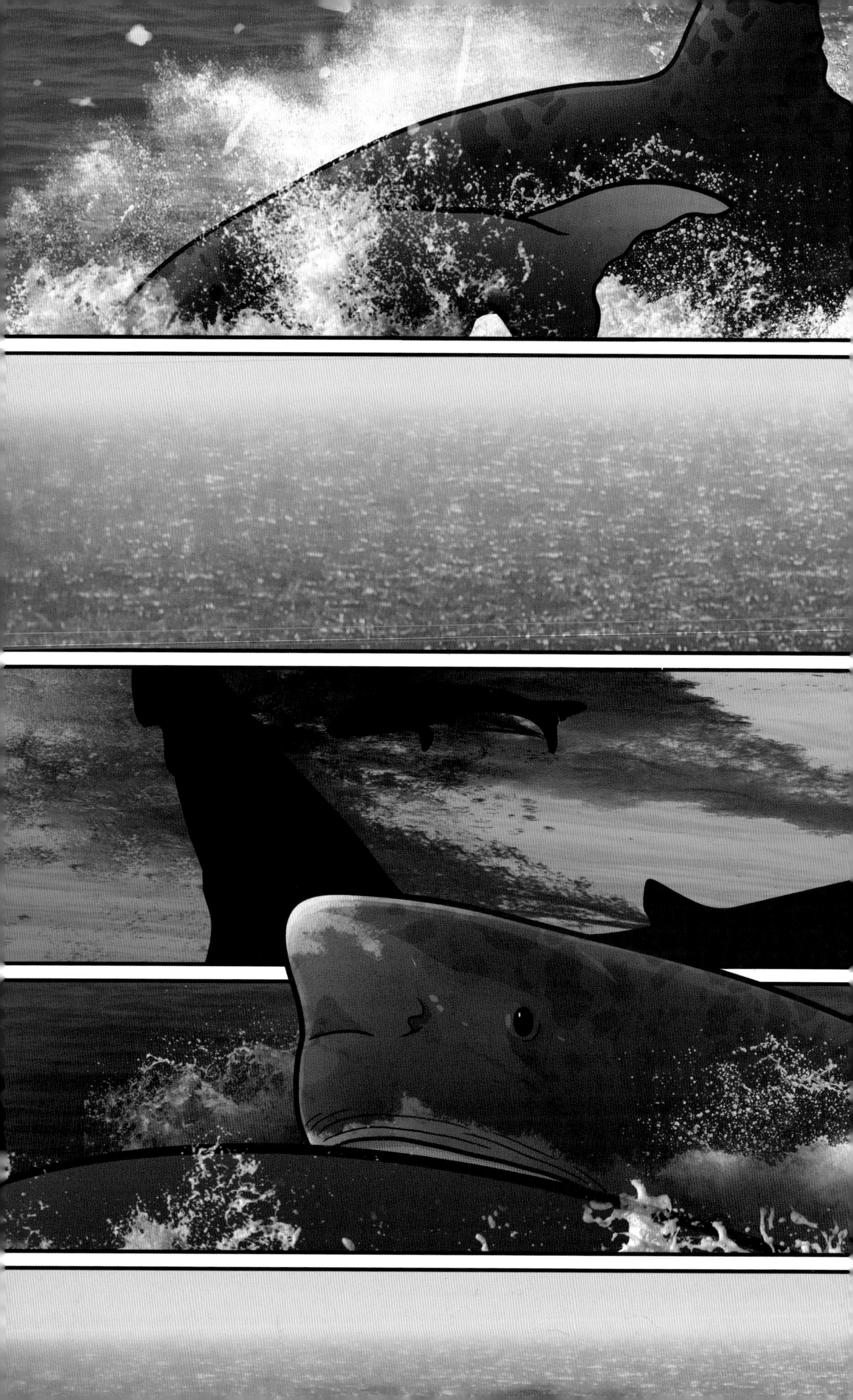

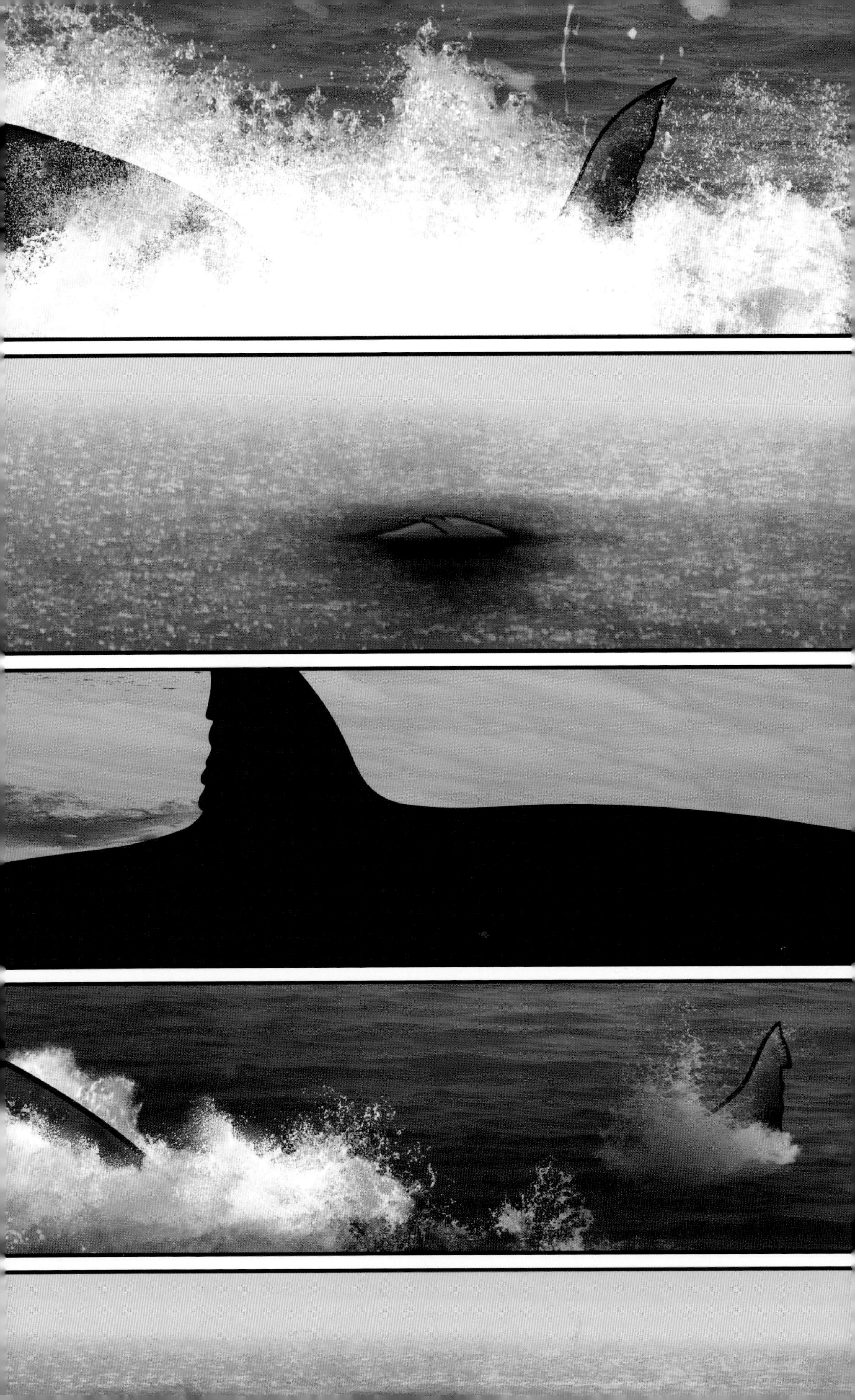

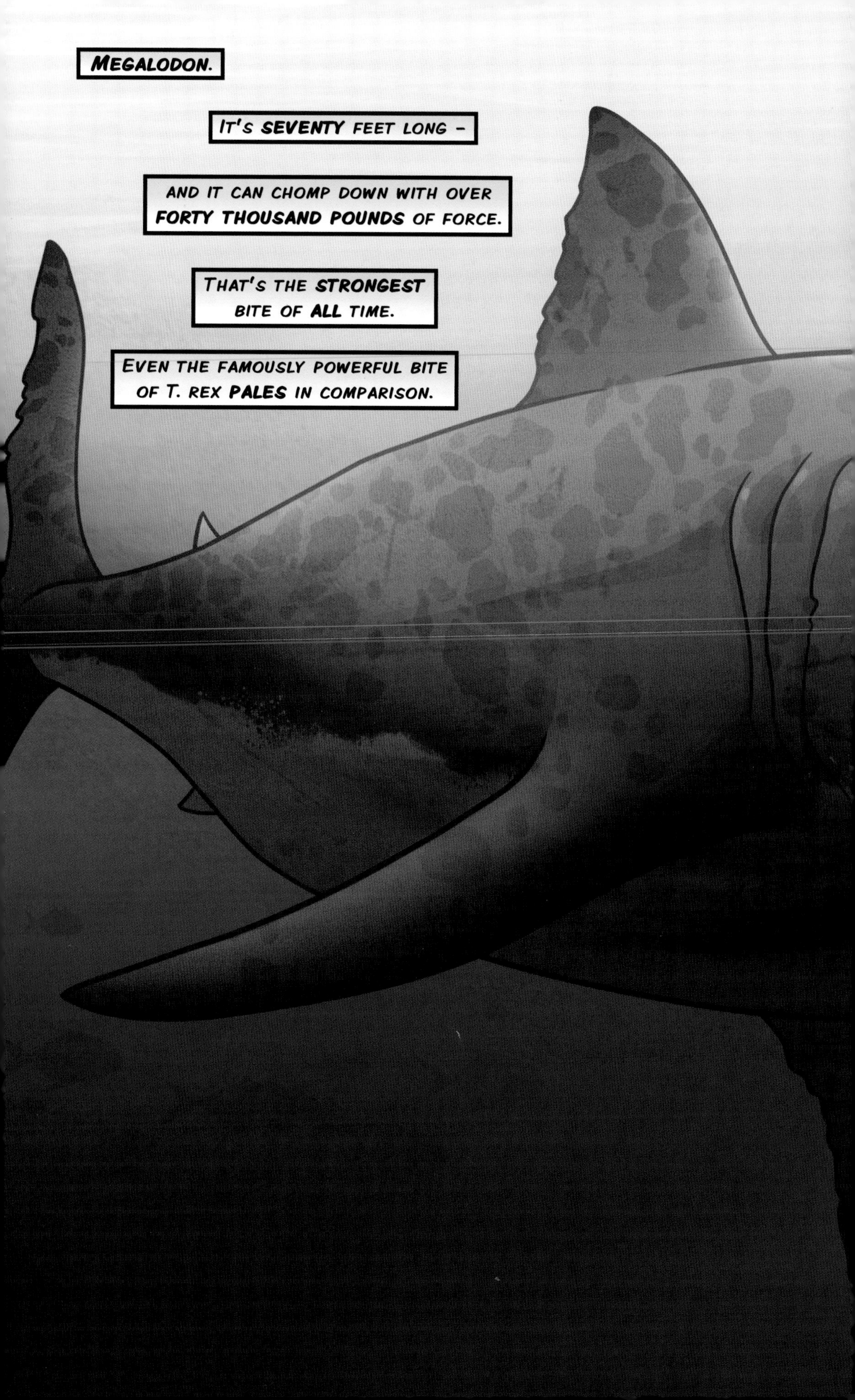
MEGALODON.
IT'S SEVENTY FEET LONG –
AND IT CAN CHOMP DOWN WITH OVER FORTY THOUSAND POUNDS OF FORCE.
THAT'S THE STRONGEST BITE OF ALL TIME.
EVEN THE FAMOUSLY POWERFUL BITE OF T. REX PALES IN COMPARISON.

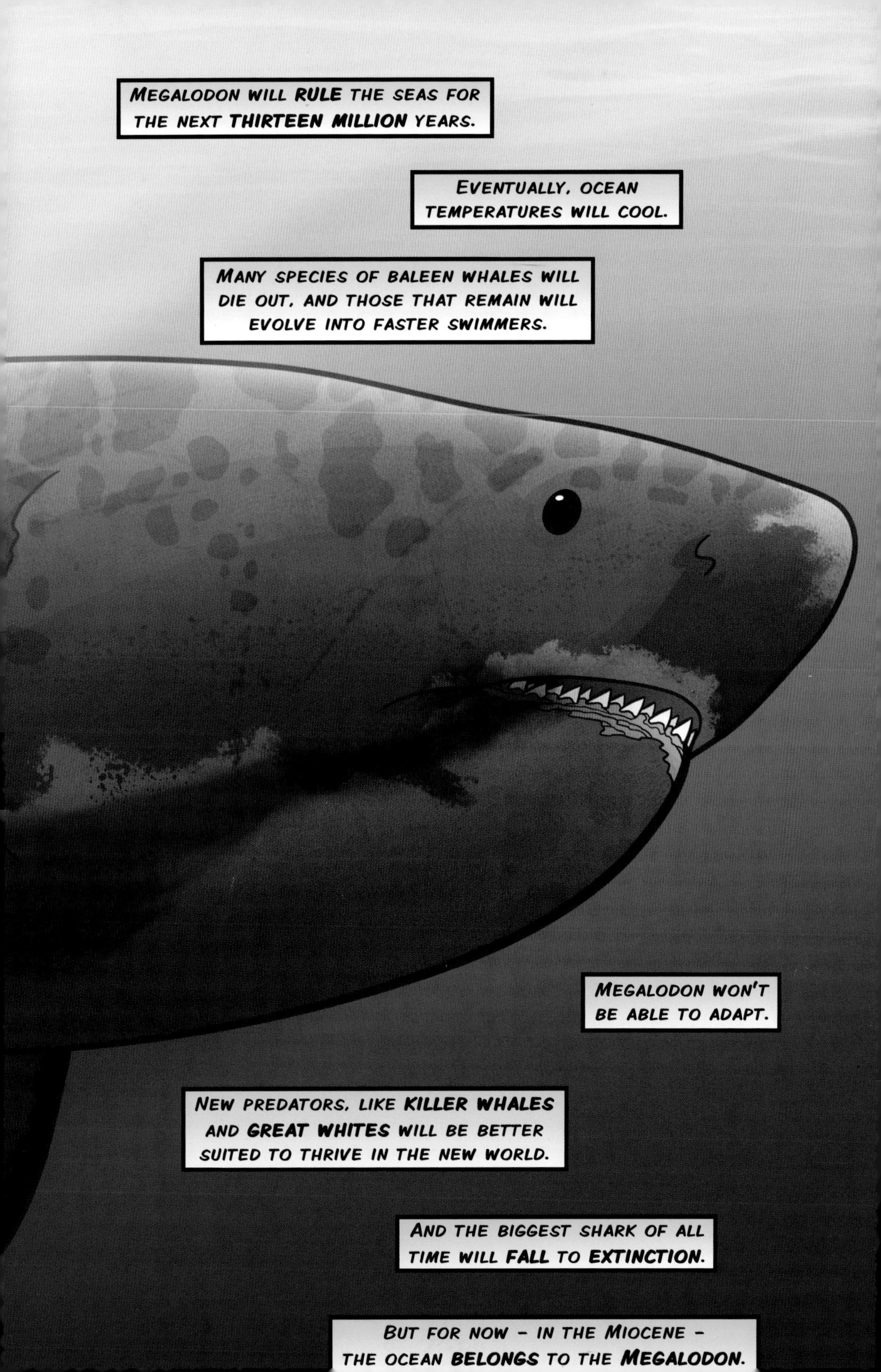
MEGALODON WILL RULE THE SEAS FOR THE NEXT THIRTEEN MILLION YEARS.
EVENTUALLY, OCEAN TEMPERATURES WILL COOL.
MANY SPECIES OF BALEEN WHALES WILL DIE OUT, AND THOSE THAT REMAIN WILL EVOLVE INTO FASTER SWIMMERS.
MEGALODON WON'T BE ABLE TO ADAPT.
NEW PREDATORS, LIKE KILLER WHALES AND GREAT WHITES WILL BE BETTER SUITED TO THRIVE IN THE NEW WORLD.
AND THE BIGGEST SHARK OF ALL TIME WILL FALL TO EXTINCTION.
BUT FOR NOW - IN THE MIOCENE - THE OCEAN BELONGS TO THE MEGALODON.

PART FOUR

NOW

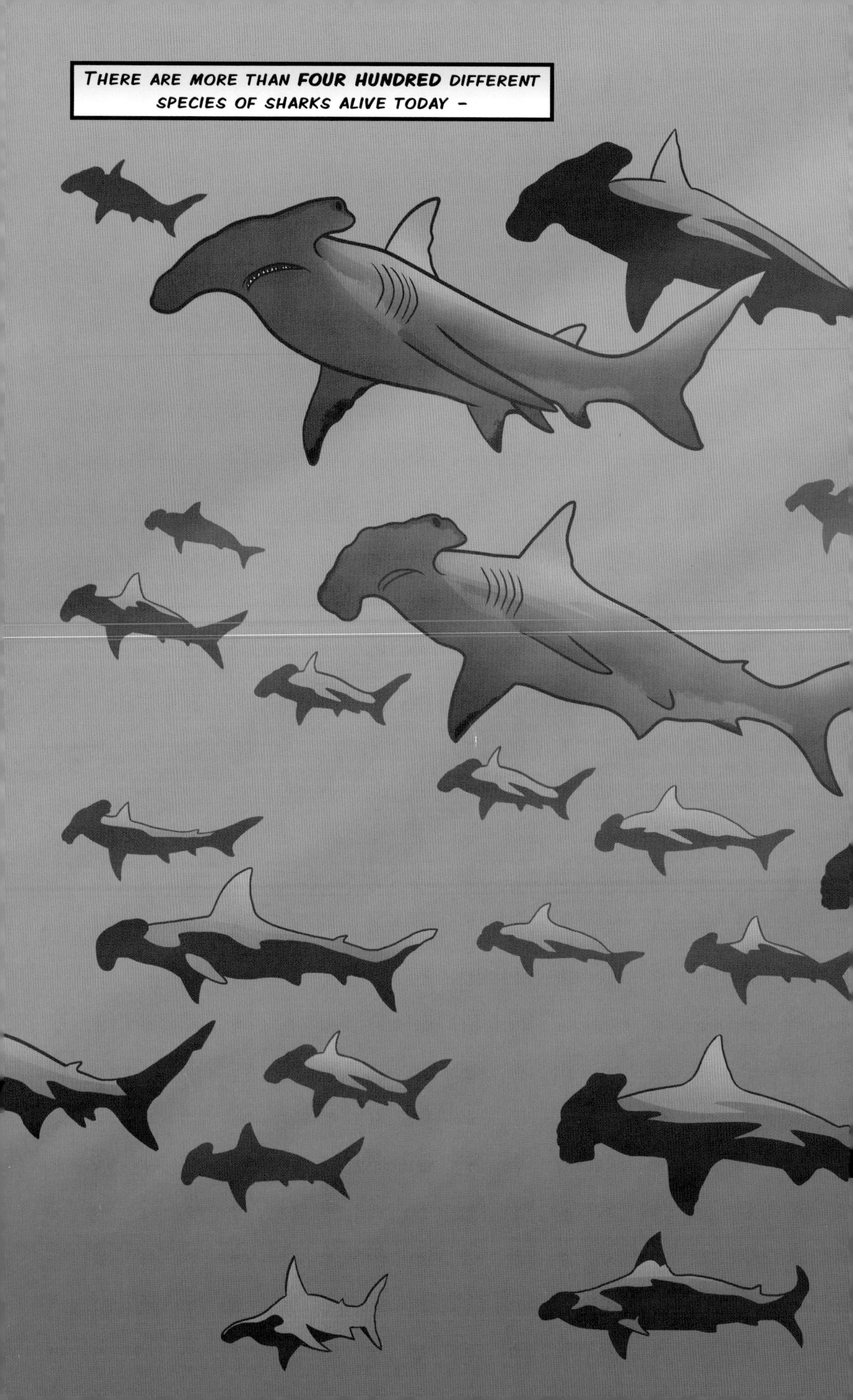
THERE ARE MORE THAN FOUR HUNDRED DIFFERENT SPECIES OF SHARKS ALIVE TODAY –

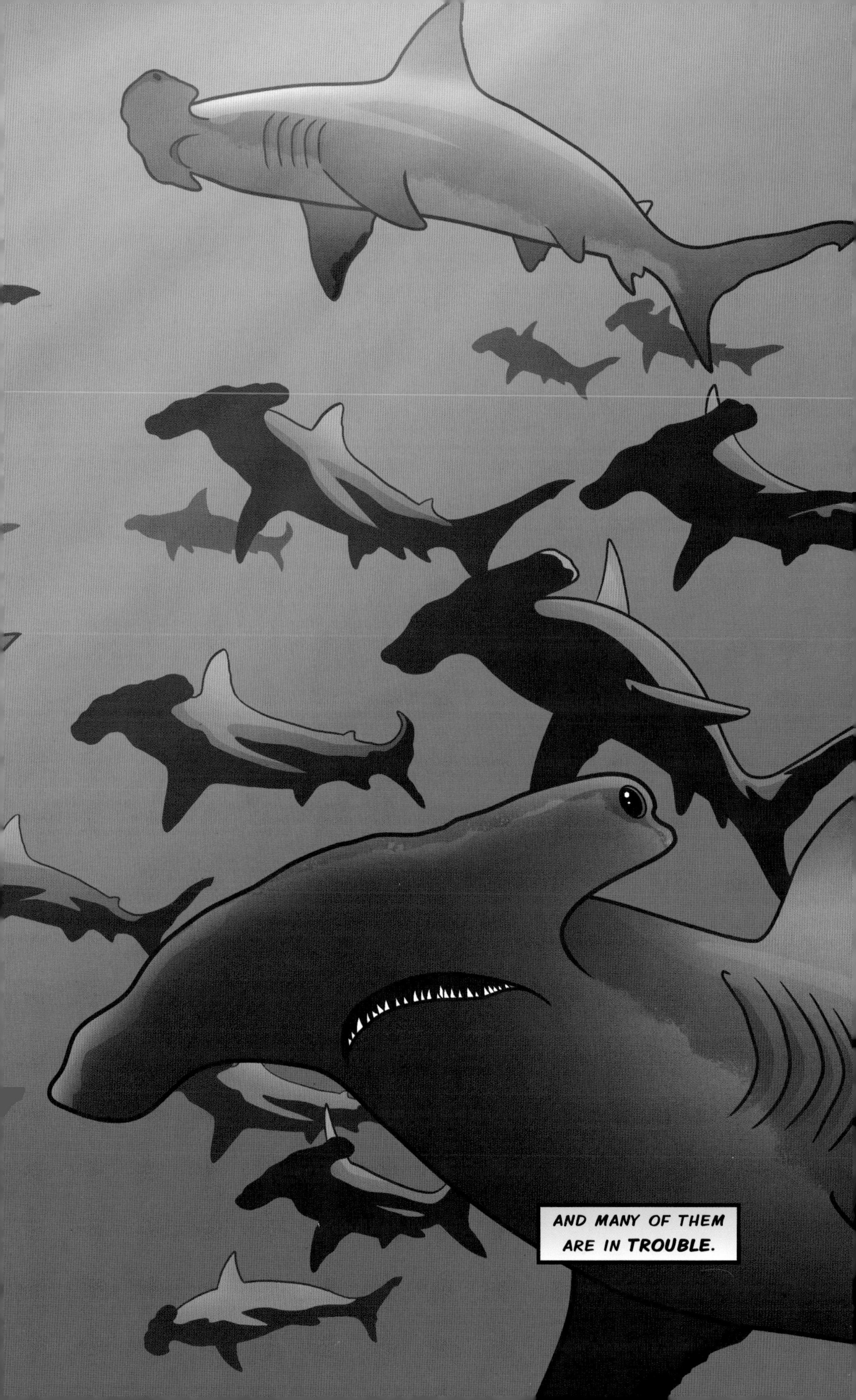
AND MANY OF THEM ARE IN TROUBLE.

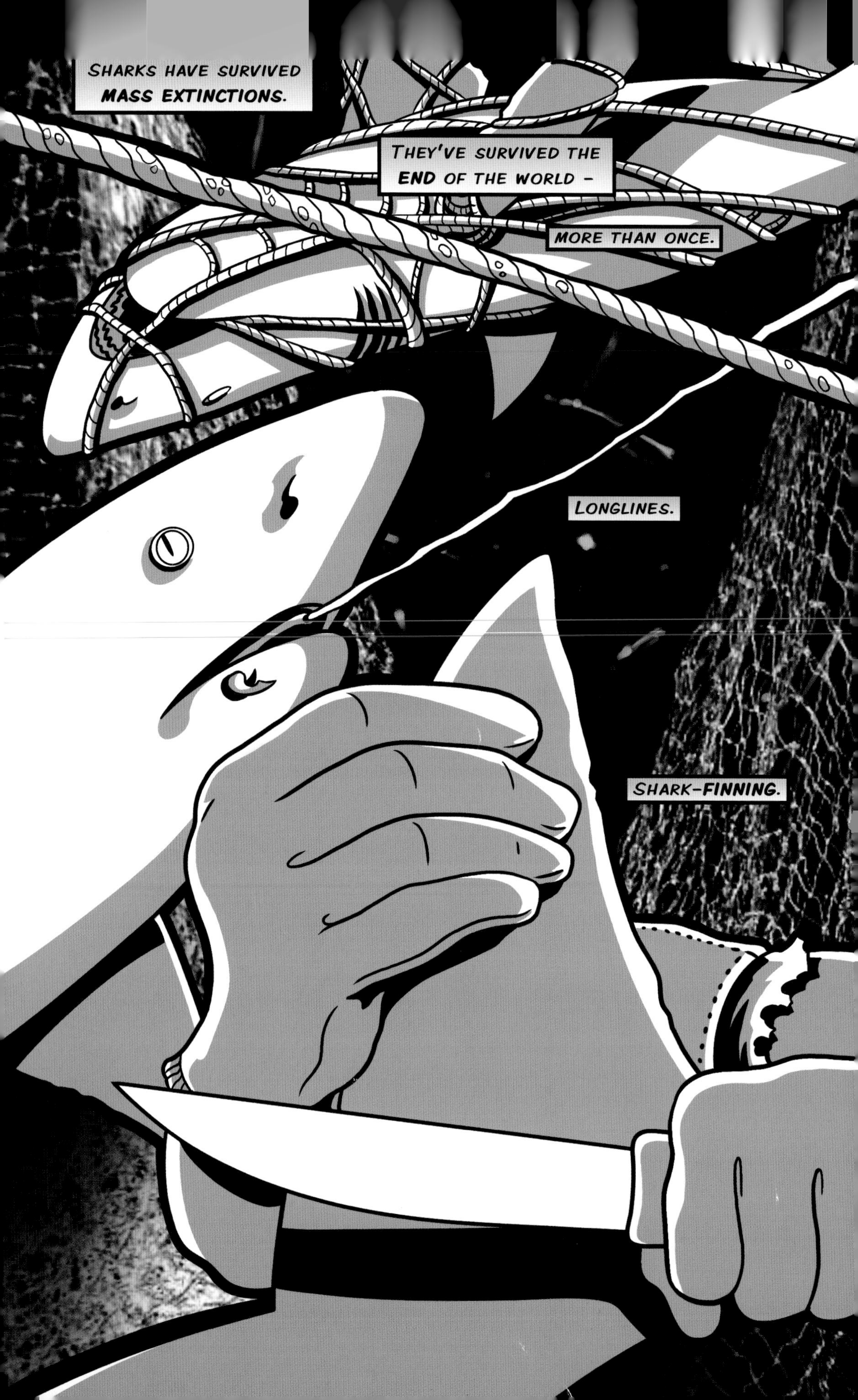

SHARKS HAVE SURVIVED MASS EXTINCTIONS.
THEY'VE SURVIVED THE END OF THE WORLD –
MORE THAN ONCE.
LONGLINES.
SHARK-FINNING.

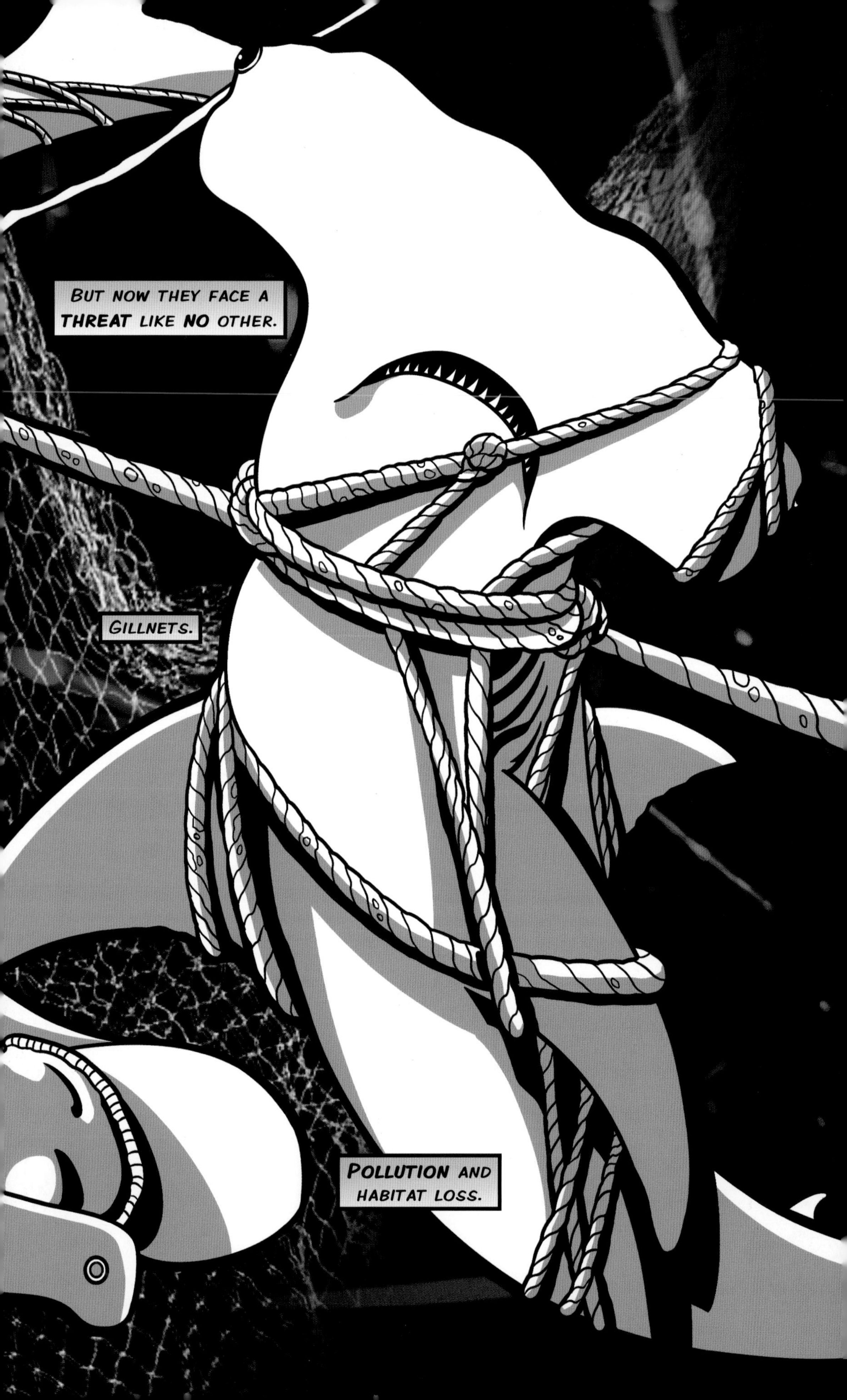
BUT NOW THEY FACE A THREAT LIKE NO OTHER.
GILLNETS.
POLLUTION AND HABITAT LOSS.

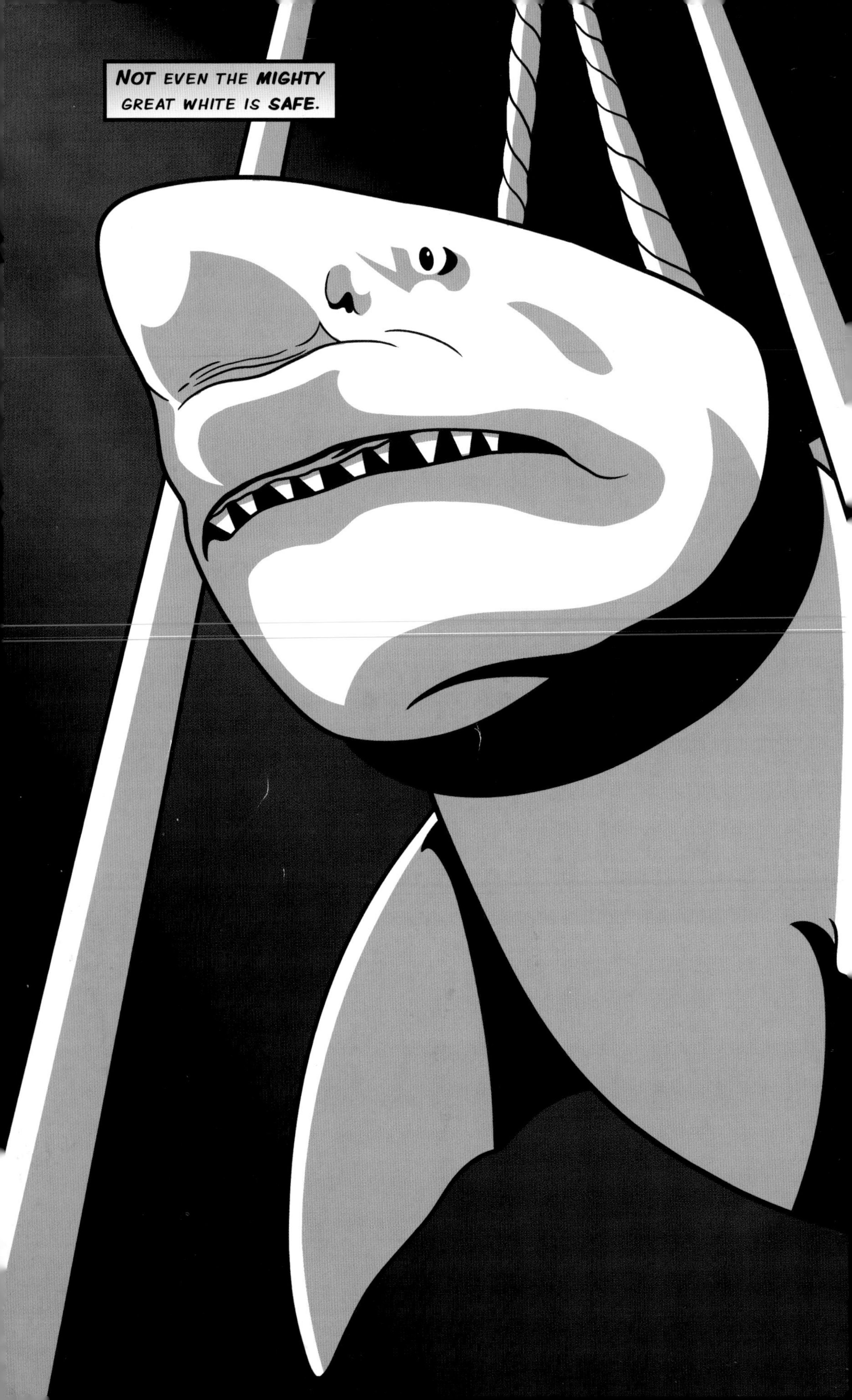
NOT EVEN THE MIGHTY GREAT WHITE IS SAFE.

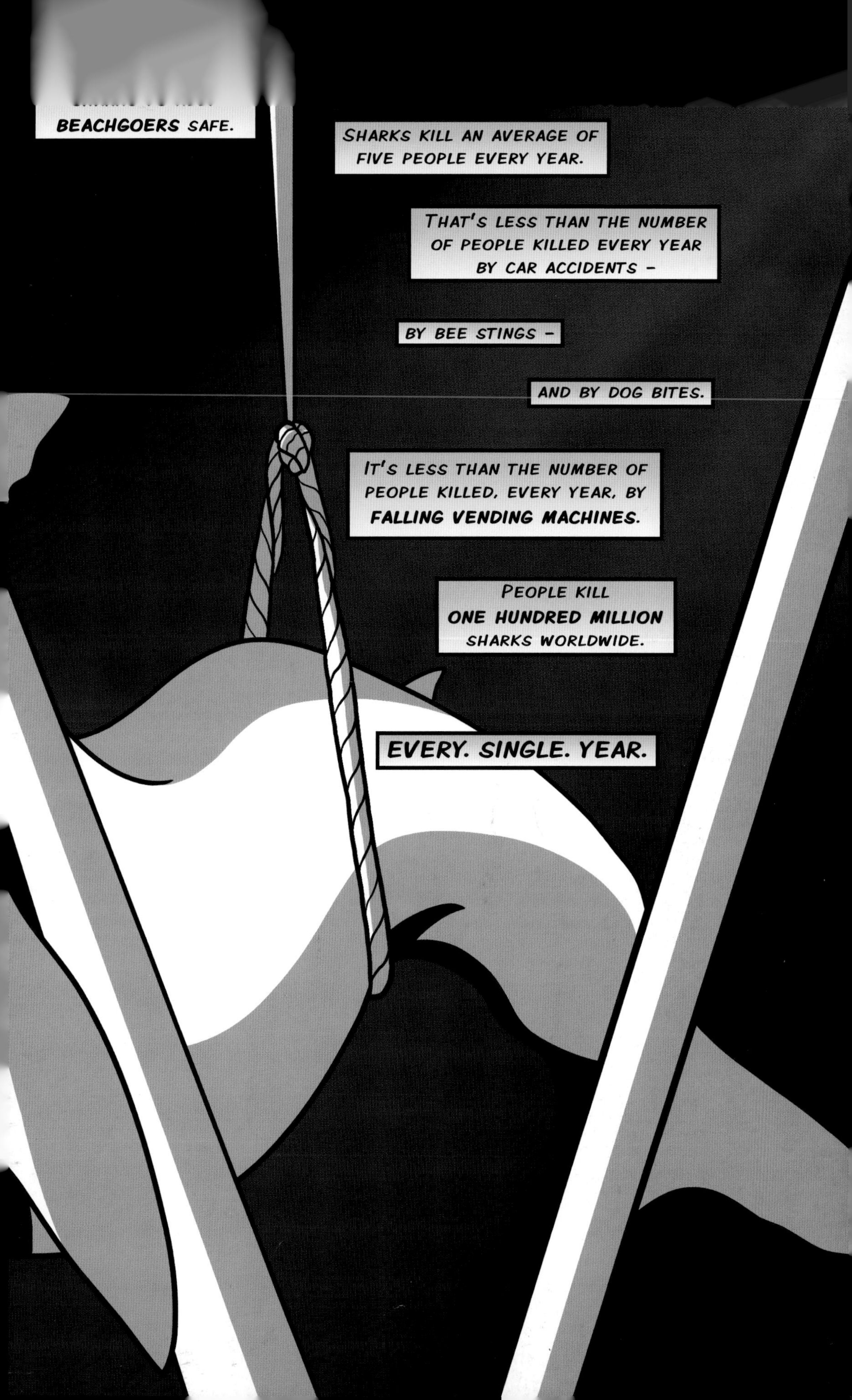
BEACHGOERS SAFE.
SHARKS KILL AN AVERAGE OF FIVE PEOPLE EVERY YEAR.
THAT'S LESS THAN THE NUMBER OF PEOPLE KILLED EVERY YEAR BY CAR ACCIDENTS –
BY BEE STINGS –
AND BY DOG BITES.
IT'S LESS THAN THE NUMBER OF PEOPLE KILLED, EVERY YEAR, BY FALLING VENDING MACHINES.
PEOPLE KILL ONE HUNDRED MILLION SHARKS WORLDWIDE.
EVERY. SINGLE. YEAR.

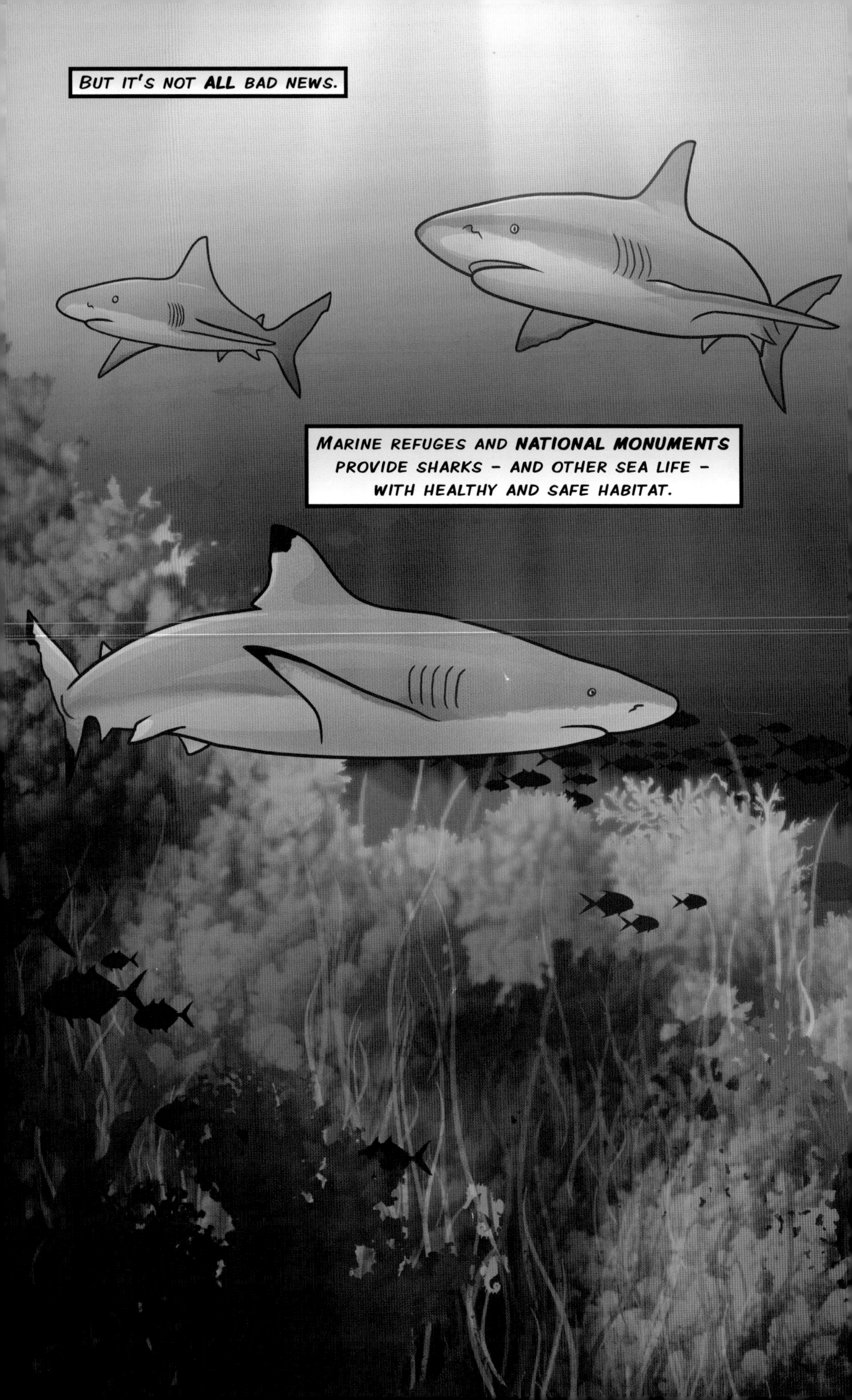
BUT IT'S NOT ALL BAD NEWS.
MARINE REFUGES AND NATIONAL MONUMENTS PROVIDE SHARKS - AND OTHER SEA LIFE - WITH HEALTHY AND SAFE HABITAT.

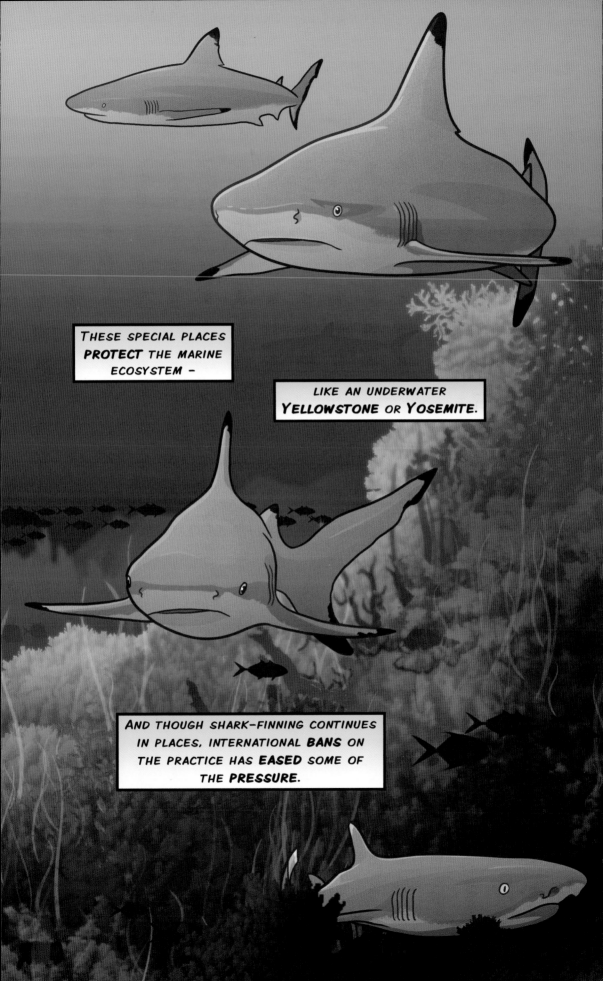

These special places **PROTECT** the marine ecosystem —

Like an underwater **Yellowstone** or **Yosemite**.

And though shark-finning continues in places, international **BANS** on the practice has **EASED** some of the **PRESSURE**.

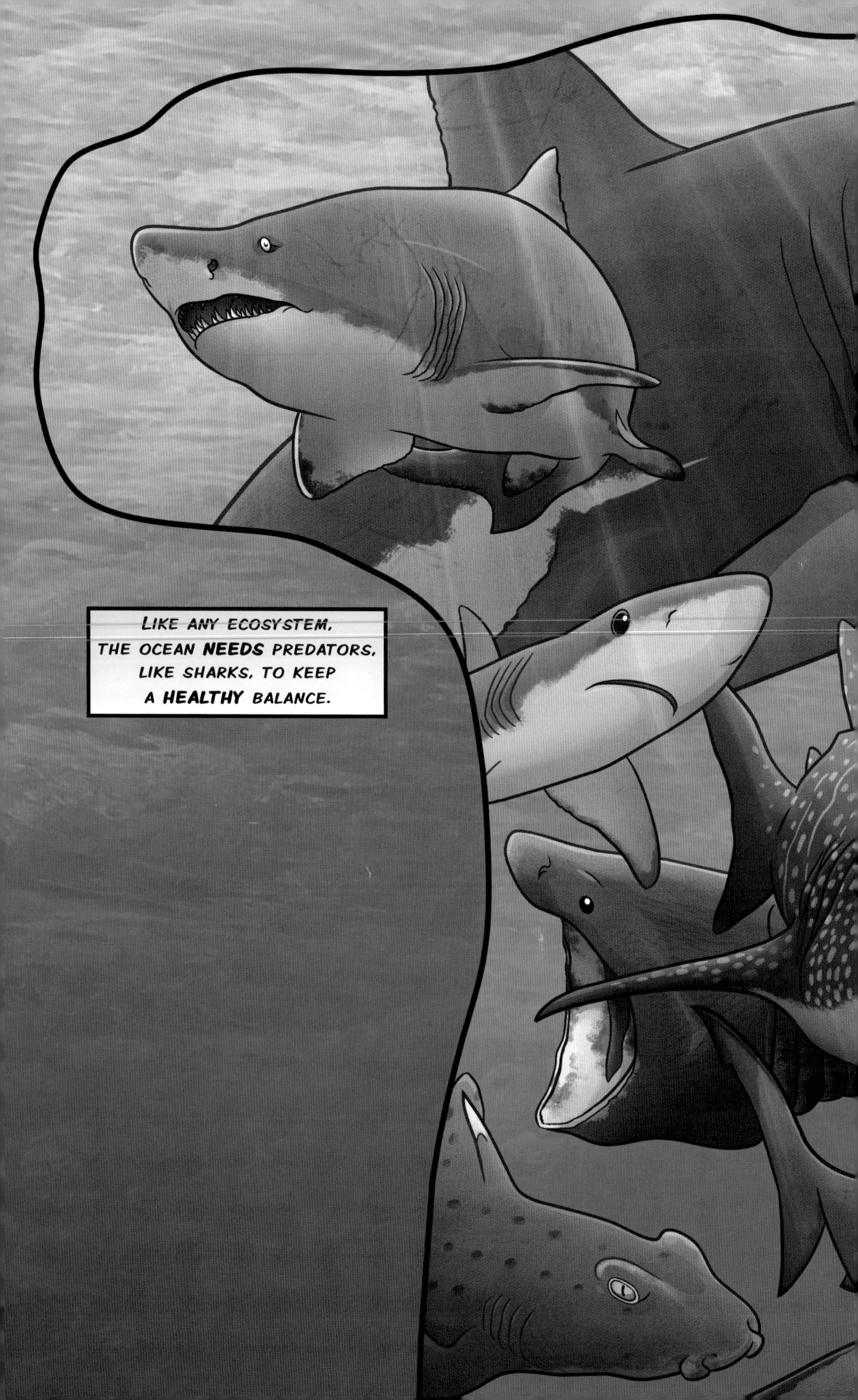
LIKE ANY ECOSYSTEM, THE OCEAN NEEDS PREDATORS, LIKE SHARKS, TO KEEP A HEALTHY BALANCE.

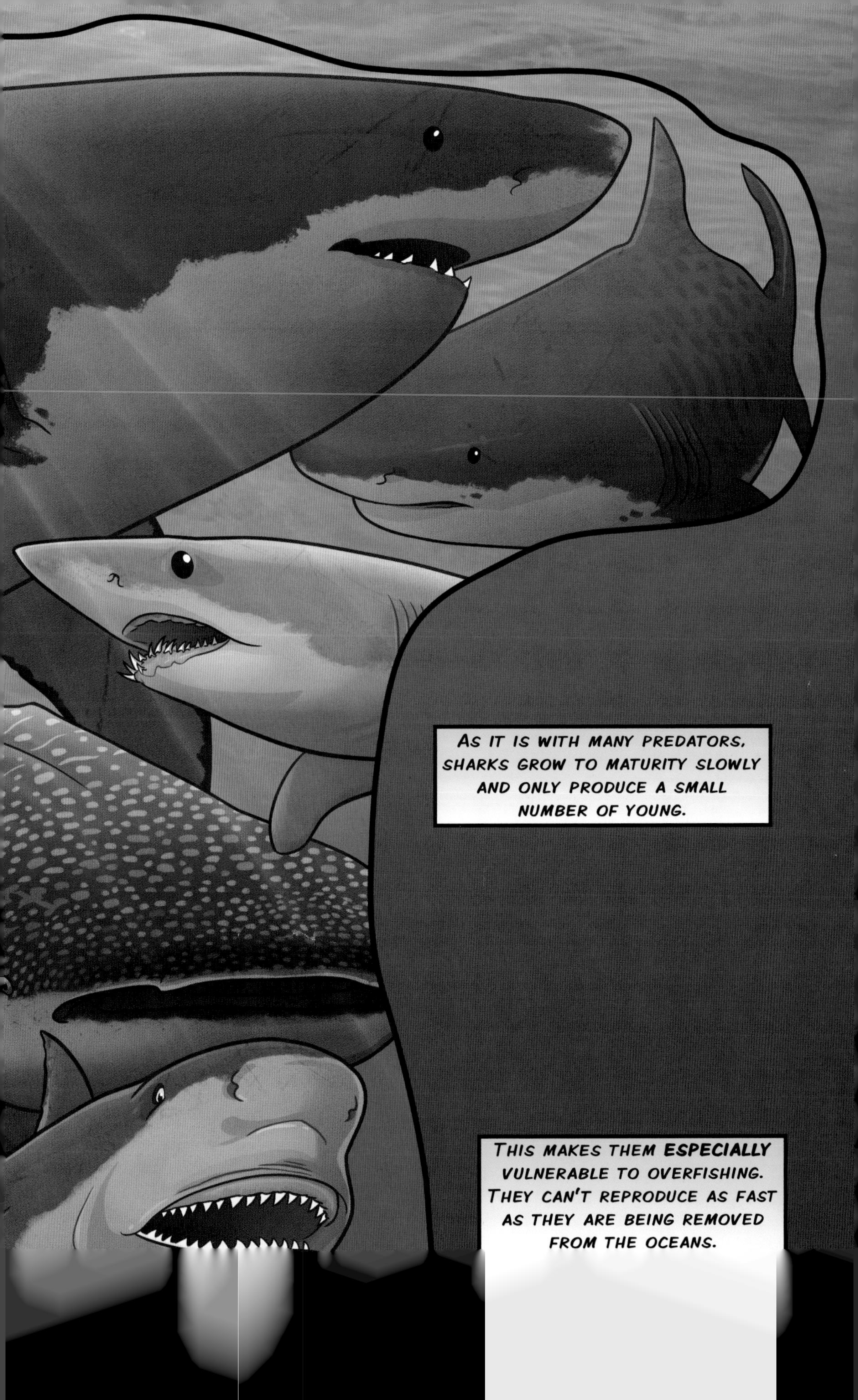
AS IT IS WITH MANY PREDATORS, SHARKS GROW TO MATURITY SLOWLY AND ONLY PRODUCE A SMALL NUMBER OF YOUNG.
THIS MAKES THEM **ESPECIALLY** VULNERABLE TO OVERFISHING. THEY CAN'T REPRODUCE AS FAST AS THEY ARE BEING REMOVED FROM THE OCEANS.

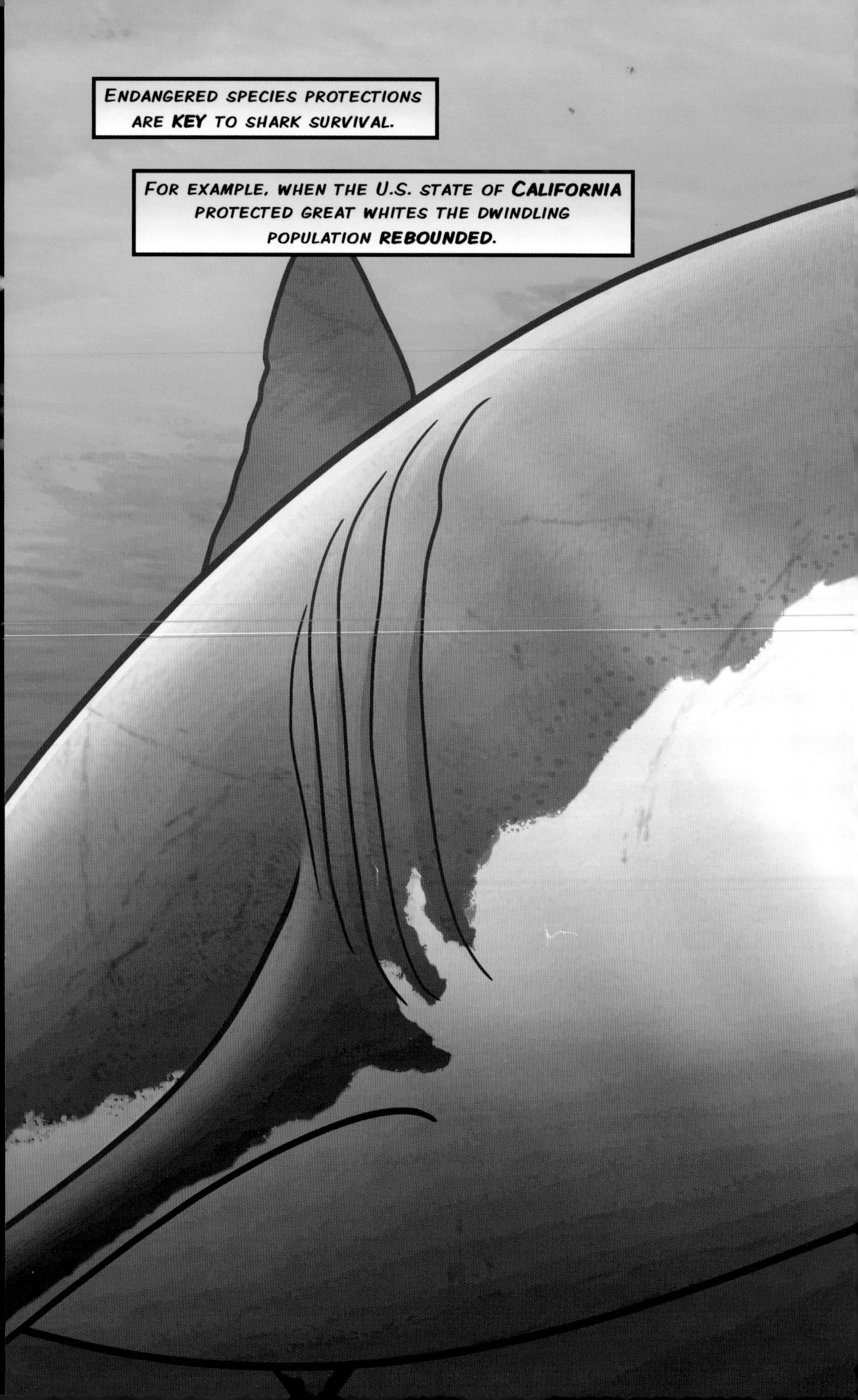
ENDANGERED SPECIES PROTECTIONS ARE KEY TO SHARK SURVIVAL.
FOR EXAMPLE, WHEN THE U.S. STATE OF CALIFORNIA PROTECTED GREAT WHITES THE DWINDLING POPULATION REBOUNDED.

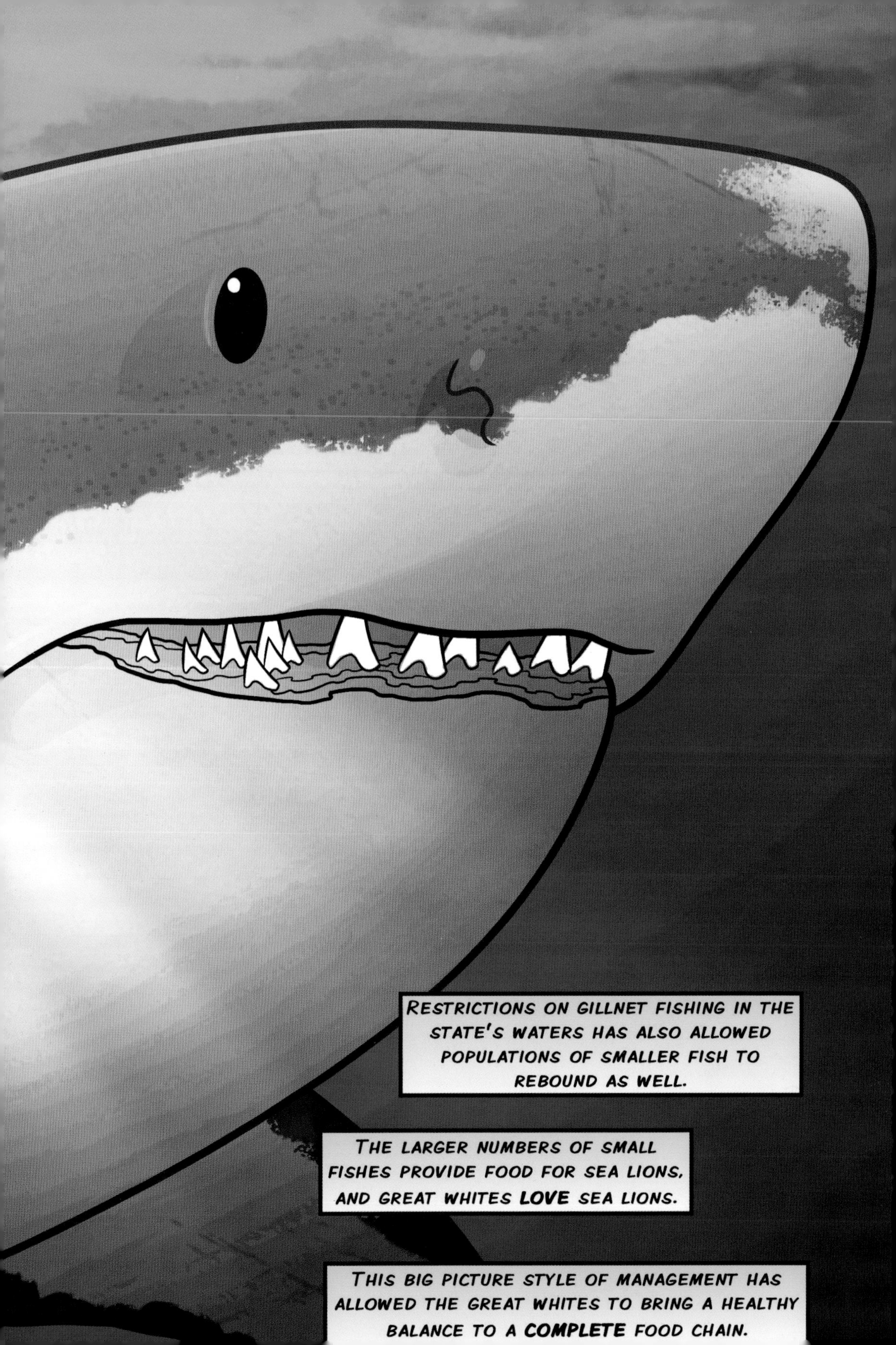
RESTRICTIONS ON GILLNET FISHING IN THE STATE'S WATERS HAS ALSO ALLOWED POPULATIONS OF SMALLER FISH TO REBOUND AS WELL.
THE LARGER NUMBERS OF SMALL FISHES PROVIDE FOOD FOR SEA LIONS, AND GREAT WHITES LOVE SEA LIONS.
THIS BIG PICTURE STYLE OF MANAGEMENT HAS ALLOWED THE GREAT WHITES TO BRING A HEALTHY BALANCE TO A COMPLETE FOOD CHAIN.

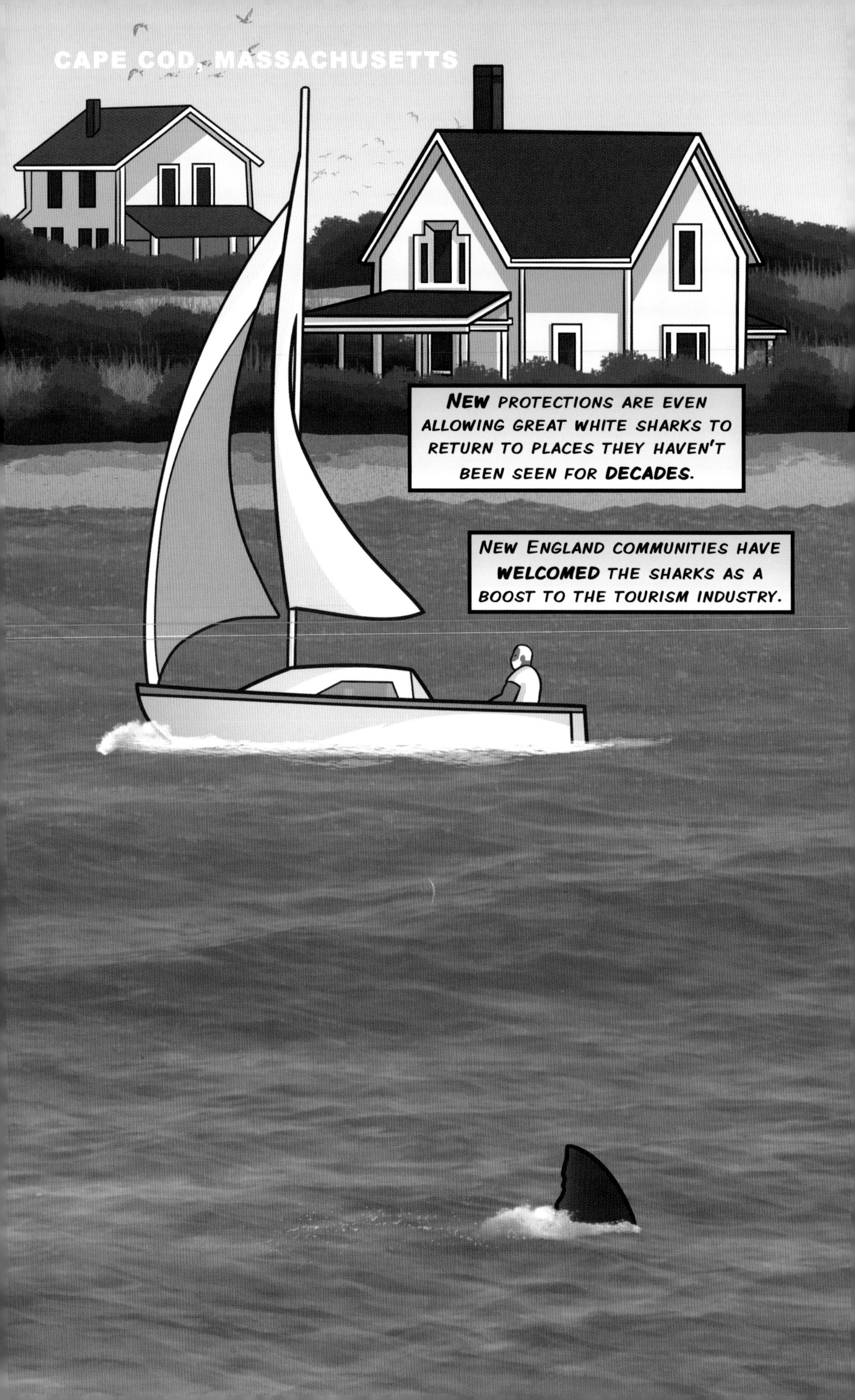
CAPE COD, MASSACHUSETTS
NEW PROTECTIONS ARE EVEN ALLOWING GREAT WHITE SHARKS TO RETURN TO PLACES THEY HAVEN'T BEEN SEEN FOR DECADES.
NEW ENGLAND COMMUNITIES HAVE WELCOMED THE SHARKS AS A BOOST TO THE TOURISM INDUSTRY.

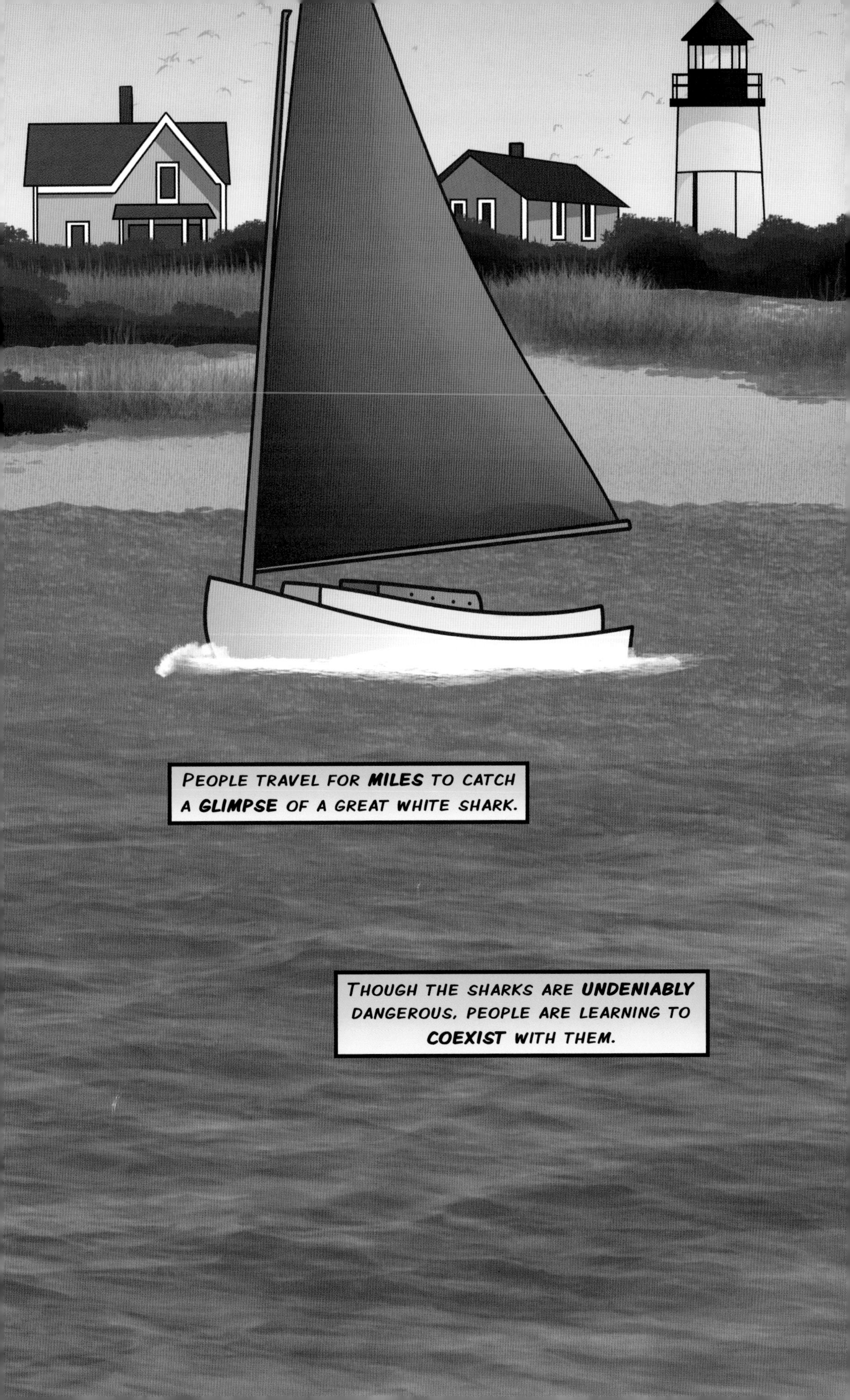
PEOPLE TRAVEL FOR MILES TO CATCH A GLIMPSE OF A GREAT WHITE SHARK.
THOUGH THE SHARKS ARE UNDENIABLY DANGEROUS, PEOPLE ARE LEARNING TO COEXIST WITH THEM.

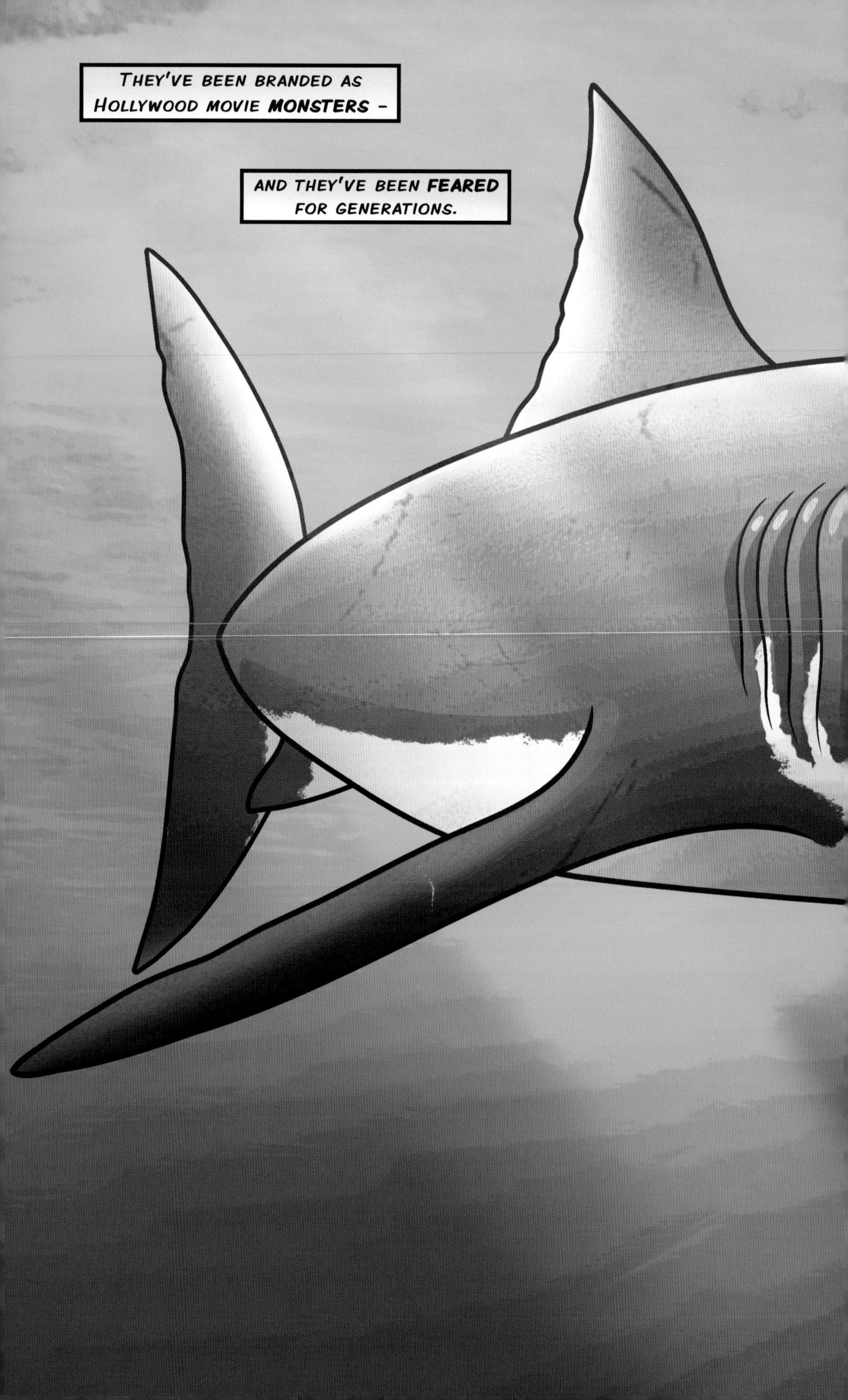
They've been branded as Hollywood movie **MONSTERS** –
and they've been **FEARED** for generations.

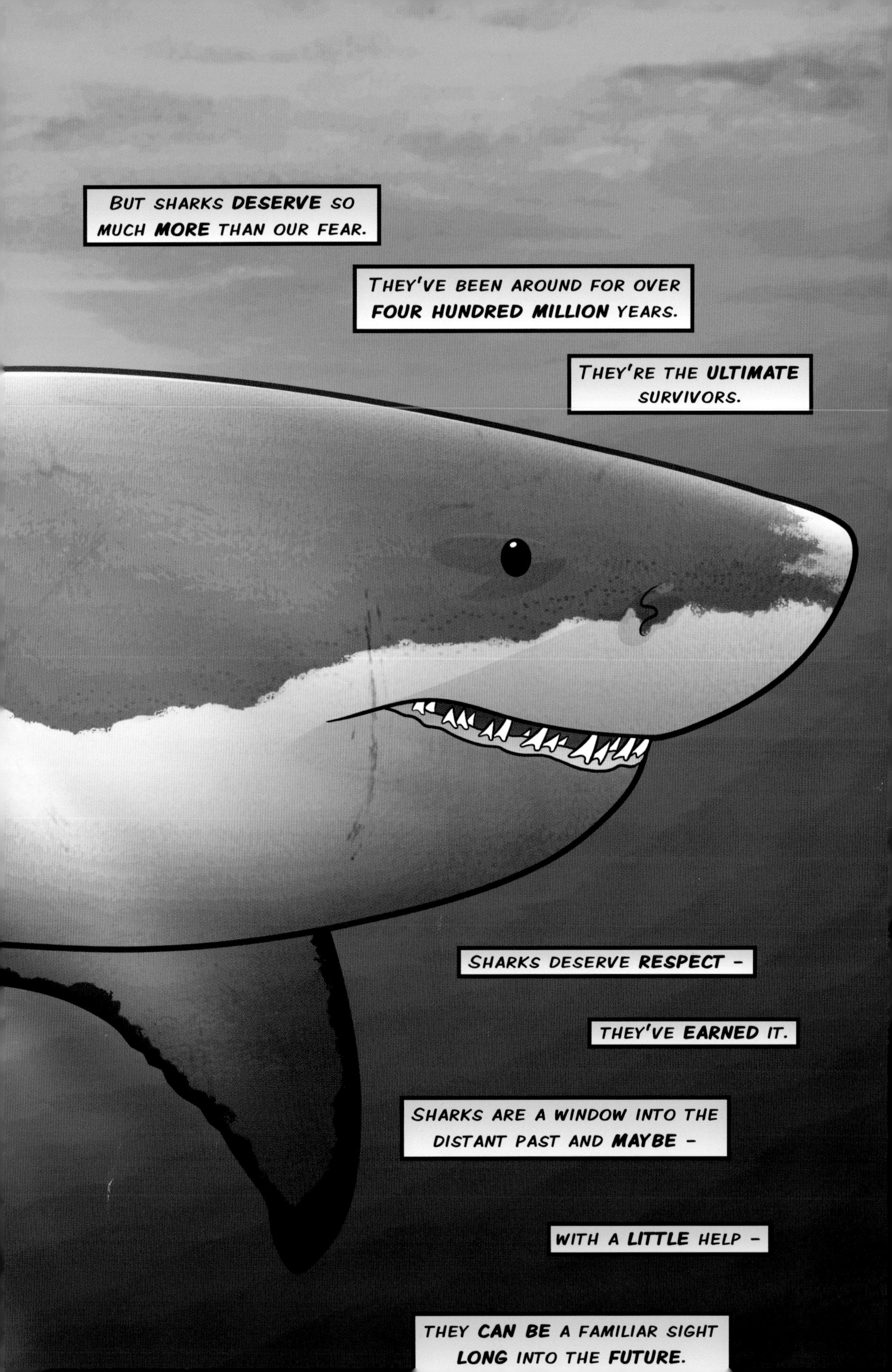
BUT SHARKS DESERVE SO MUCH MORE THAN OUR FEAR.
THEY'VE BEEN AROUND FOR OVER FOUR HUNDRED MILLION YEARS.
THEY'RE THE ULTIMATE SURVIVORS.
SHARKS DESERVE RESPECT –
THEY'VE EARNED IT.
SHARKS ARE A WINDOW INTO THE DISTANT PAST AND MAYBE –
WITH A LITTLE HELP –
THEY CAN BE A FAMILIAR SIGHT LONG INTO THE FUTURE.

REXTOOTH
STUDIOS
REXTOOTH.COM

MORE BOOKS BY TED RECHLIN

BEARS
TED RECHLIN

TYRANNOSAURUS REX
TED RECHLIN
FOREWORD BY
@SUEtheTrex

JURASSIC
TED RECHLIN

Look for these titles at your local store, online, or at Rextooth.com.

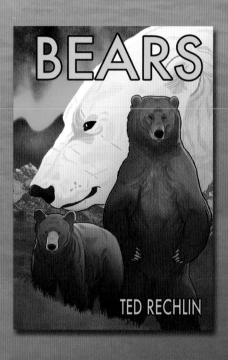

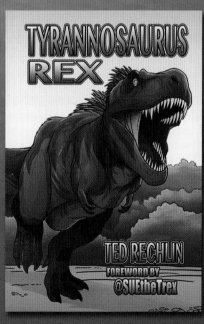

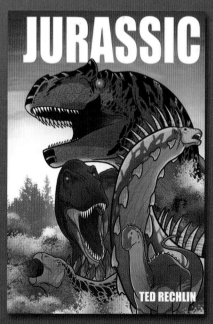

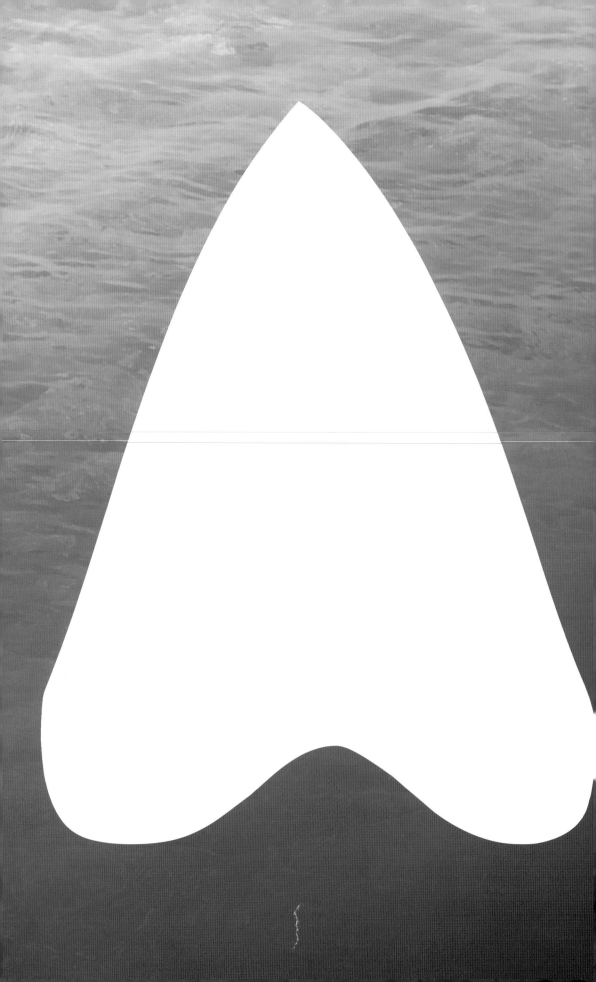